GAME 4 $ALE
THE HUSTLER'S BIBLE

Kamaj Tawhid

Still Waters Prose
Albuquerque, NM

Copyright © 2025 by Still Waters Prose, LLC
All rights reserved.

www.StillWatersProse.com
Library of Congress Cataloging-in-Publication Data is available upon request.

ISBN
978-1-7355890-6-0 (First hardcover printing)
978-1-7355890-7-7 (First paperback printing)
978-1-7355890-8-4 (Ebook epub version)
978-1-7355890-9-1 (Audiobook version)

PRINTED IN THE UNITED STATES OF AMERICA
Cover design by agnesam
Book design by accuracy4sure

First hardcover / paperback / audio / ebook edition 2025
www.Game4$ale.com
www.TheHustlersBible.com

Dedication

This book is dedicated to every hustler who ever thought survival was the only way. To the children who carried scars they never asked for. To the families broken by "the game"—and to the ones strong enough to break the cycle.

To my loved ones, blood and chosen, whom have stood by me as the system has tried to erase me. To my sons, stepsons, goddaughters, nephews, nieces, lil cousins, and *every* other child who deserves a present parent. To my ancestors and big homies, whose struggles I carry, and whose strength keeps me unbroken.

This is for the misunderstood, the misrepresented, and the misjudged. For those whom society calls criminals, but history will call survivors. For anyone ready to turn pain into power, hustle into healing, and survival into legacy.

Last but not least, this is for my father Milton, my brother CaCa, my cousin Raymond, and the homies Bert Train, Devo, C-Lo, Cash Flow, Babylon, and Gangsta Grimm.

Foreword

When I first met Kamaj, back when I knew him as Delo, freedom was the heartbeat of our conversations. He wasn't just talking about it—he lived it. He stood firm on his principles, willing to sacrifice everything rather than compromise what he believed to be true. His petition to the government, "Give me liberty or give me death," wasn't a slogan. It was a vow. That spirit shaped the man and laid the foundation for the book you now hold.

There's an old saying: "Give a man a fish, and you feed him for a day. Teach a man to fish, and you feed him for a lifetime." Kamaj takes that wisdom and elevates it. In *Game 4 $ale: The Hustler's Bible,* he doesn't just teach you how to fish—he shows you how to build the boat, read the waters, and navigate toward something greater. He exposes the trap of the hustle while pointing toward the power of legacy.

What you'll find here isn't just a collection of lessons—it's lived truth. It's the voice of someone who's carried the weight of survival and still chose to transform that struggle into a blueprint for others. Kamaj doesn't glamorize "the game"; he dissects it. And in doing so, he offers an alternative: growth, peace, and generational impact.

So, as you turn these pages, remember this: anyone can chase money, but few can build meaning. What you build today will echo tomorrow—through your children, your community, and your legacy. Kamaj has written his truth. Now it's on you to take it, learn from it, and decide what story you'll leave behind.

by Rivera L. Peoples
Author of *Power vs. Poverty: Following the Money to Reveal America's Mass Incarceration Scheme*

Foreword

There's no shortage of books claiming to teach "game." You'll find them everywhere—quick fixes, empty slogans, and recycled advice. But *Game 4 $ale* is something different. It's not theory, and it's not an outsider's perspective—it's written *by* a hustler *for* hustlers. It's the lived truth of a man who's walked the walk, paid the price, and chosen to turn his experience into wisdom. Furthermore, this isn't just a book about hustling—it's about evolving beyond it.

I had the privilege of watching *The Hustler's Bible* come to life from the very beginning, and I can say without hesitation: this isn't just another title on the shelf. It's a blueprint. It's real, it's raw, and it's necessary. Kamaj writes with the kind of authority that only comes from survival, reflection, and vision. He doesn't glorify "the game"—he breaks it down, exposes its traps, and offers a way forward.

If you already have game, these pages will sharpen it. If you don't, they'll teach you more than technique—they'll teach you perspective. And if you're ready for something beyond the hustle, this book gives you the mindset to move toward legacy. That's what makes *Game 4 $ale* more than a book—it's a lifeline. A must-read for anyone serious about growth, purpose, and impact.

by **M. Deuce**
**Author of *The Coldest Game*
& *Rats vs. Snakes***

Author's Note on Language & Style

Straight up, I don't write by *their* "rules"—I write how *I* talk, how *I* think, and how *I've* lived. Grammar books can't define *my* story, and "polished" sentences can't capture the raw truth of where *I've* been. What you see on these pages is uncut and intentional—*my* rhythm, *my* cadence, *my* voice.

Dig that *any* book you get from me ain't about looking pretty on paper—it's about being real. It's about telling *my* truth the way it comes out of *me*, without filters, without "correction," without apology.

So, read *Game 4 $ale* how it's written, and feel it how it's meant. Because what's here isn't dressed up for *their* "approval"—it's carved out of survival, sharpened by struggle, and delivered in a voice that refuses to be silenced. This is for you…

Contents

Dedication iii
Foreword v
Foreword vii
Author's Note on Language & Style ix
Introduction 1
Chapter 1: The Hustle Was Never Just About Money 3
    A Way Out... and a Way In 4
    More Than Money, Less Than Peace 5
    The Unseen Toll 6
Chapter 2: What Makes a Hustler? 9
    The Anatomy of a Hustler 9
        Survivor's Mindset 9
        Hyper-Responsibility 10
        Emotional Armor 10
        Calculated Risk 11
    Not Every Hustle Looks the Same 11
    Addicted to the Struggle 11
    You Don't Need to Lose Your Hustle—You Need to Rewire It 12
Chapter 3: The Hidden Costs of "the Game" 15
    The Time You'll Never Get Back 15
    The People Who Paid with You 16
    The Self You Had to Bury 17
    The Illusion of Control 17
    The Loneliness That "Success" Can't Fix 18
    Pain Isn't the Price of Purpose 19
Chapter 4: You Can't Hustle Your Way to Healing 21
    Hustling Is a Trauma Response 21

Pain Doesn't Disappear—It Multiplies 22
Rest Isn't Weakness—It's Recovery 23
Letting Go of the Mask 23
Healing Doesn't Make You Soft—It Makes You Solid 24
Setting Up Chapters 5-10 25

Chapter 5: Why Hustling Isn't Compatible with Relationships or Parenthood 27

The Hustler's Love Dilemma 27
   The Nature of "the Game" 28
   Survival Mode vs. Intimacy 29
   Trust and Transparency: A Dangerous Game 30
   The Illusion of Stability 32
   Emotional Labor and Burden 33
   A Case for Timing, Not Rejection 34

Why "the Game" Shouldn't Involve Parenthood—Yet 36
   The Illusion of Providing 37
   The Trauma is Generational 38
   Time is a Currency Too 40
   Parenthood Without Peace Is a Setup 41
   A Hard Pause, Not a Permanent No 42

The Selflessness of Healing and Choosing Legacy Over "the Game" 43

Chapter 6: From Hustler to Legacy Builder—Life After "the Game" 47

The Silence After the Noise 47
You Are Not "the Game" 48
Freedom Isn't Fast—It's Built 49
You're Allowed to Start Small 50
"The Game" Has an Expiration Date 51
You Already Have the Skillset—Now Redirect It 52
Turning Respect into Influence 53
Rewriting the Narrative 54

What Legacy Really Means 55
The Next Chapter Is Yours to Write 56

Chapter 7: Exit Strategies, Financial Literacy & Long-Term Wealth for Former Hustlers 59

Fast Money vs. Free Money: Fast Money Has No Foundation 60
What "the Streets" Don't Teach You About Money 61
    Cash Flow Isn't the Same as Wealth 61
    Income Without Structure Is a Setup 62
    You Can't Out-Earn Financial Illiteracy 63
    Ownership Over Flex: Assets vs. Liabilities 65
    Wealth Without Healing Is Just a Fancier Cage 69
Breaking Emotional Generational Curses 70
The Wealth Tools You Were Never Taught 71
    Budgeting Is Strategy, Not Scarcity 71
    Credit Is Leverage 71
    Savings & Emergency Funds = Survival Kit 72
    Investing 72
    Business Structuring 73
New Goals, New Game 73
    Entrepreneurship—From Street CEO to Legit Boss 74
    Creative Outlets—Turning Pain into Power 75
    Mentorship—Be the Person You Needed 75
Choosing the Right Path for You 76

Chapter 8: The Mask We Wear—Mental Wellness, Emotional Recovery, and the Inner Work of Breaking Generational Curses 79

The Shit We Carry 80
You Were Lied To: Healing Is Not Weakness 80
What "Therapy" (or Self-Work) Really Looks Like 82
Generational Curses Aren't Spells—They're Patterns 83
Love in a World That Doesn't Trust it 84

Healing Is Slow—Stay with It Anyway 84
Community or Competition? 85
Mental Unwellness: The Silent Killer 86
Creating New Norms in Old Spaces 88
The Strength to Feel 88

Chapter 9: Mentorship, Leadership, and Leaving "The Streets" Better Than You Found Them 91

You Don't Have to Be a Saint to Lead 91
But Stop Selling Cats the Lie You Survived 92
Transforming "the Hood" 93
Transforming Hearts and Minds 95
Legal Livelihoods & Community Support 96
Legacy Over Clout 97

Chapter 10: Rewriting Your "Rep"—Self, Spirit, and the New You . 99

The Hustle Built a Mask, Not a Mirror 99
Reclaiming Your Name 100
Community: From Territory to Tribe 100
A Spiritual Shift (Even If You Don't Call It That) 101
Defining Success in Your Own Language 102

Epilogue: A Call to Arms 105

Acknowledgments 109

Recommended Reading 111

A Talk I Had with Some Young Cats I Know 113

AUTHOR BIO 115

Introduction

Why I Wrote *Game 4 $ale: The Hustler's Bible*

I didn't set out to write this book to glorify hustling—never that. I wrote it because I know what it feels like to live in a world where survival itself *is* the hustle. Where the rules are crooked, the deck is stacked, and the only way to breathe is to learn a "game" that was never meant for you to win.

For years, I watched young cats—and even myself, my brothers, my lil cousins and homeboys—get seduced by the surface shine of "the game." Fast money. Respect. Status. But what nobody talks about loud enough are the traps, the losses, the weight of broken promises, the families torn apart, and the prison gates waiting at the end of too many wrong turns. "The game" isn't just about money—it's about life decisions. And decisions, once made, shape destinies.

I've lived through betrayal, wrongful conviction, and the kinds of trials that make a man question not just his future, but his very soul. But through all of that, one truth has never left me: knowledge is the most powerful hustle of all. "Game"—the wisdom that comes from experience, struggle, and vision—is priceless. It can build empires, protect families, and even save lives.

That's why I wrote *Game 4 $ale: The Hustler's Bible.* Not as a manual for trapping, but as a scripture for survival, strategy, elevation, and healing. It's for the ones who feel boxed in by their circumstances, but still have the heart and mind to rise above. It's for the hustlers of every kind—in "the streets," in the boardrooms, in the courts of law and public opinion—who need a blueprint for navigating a system designed to exploit them.

My first book, *This is Amerikkka: The Troublesome Life, Loves & Soul of a Conscientious Thug*, told my story. This book tells the *lessons* that story taught me. If that memoir was about where I've been, this one is about where I'm going—and where I hope you'll go, too.

So, understand this: every page in this book is more than words. It's a weapon. It's a shield. It's a key. It's medicine. And I'm offering it not to impress you, but to prepare you. Because in a world where everything is seemingly for sale, the most valuable thing you can buy is "game."

Welcome to *The Hustler's Bible*.

Kamaj Tawhid

Chapter 1

The Hustle Was Never Just About Money

People love to romanticize hustling and the hustle.

They see it in music videos and movies—fast cars, fast cash, the sharp-tongued charisma of the street-smart cat whom makes something out of nothing. They see the success, but not the scars. They quote "get it how you get it by any means," like that shit is scripture, but they don't know what those means really cost.

Ask anyone who's really lived it—day in, day out—and they'll tell you: *The hustle was never just about money.*

It was about survival.

It was about power.

It was about control in a world that kept making you feel small.

It was about making something move when everything around you felt stuck.

And sometimes, it was about trying to fill a hole so deep you stopped believing it could be filled at all.

Let's be clear: the hustle is a response to deprivation.

Deprivation of opportunities.

Deprivation of stability.

Deprivation of safety.

Deprivation of identity…

If no one ever gave you a lane, you *made* one.

If the world never handed you a title, you named *your goddamned self*.

If the system didn't offer you structure, you built your own—but it was fragile, dangerous, and temporary.

And that's what people on the outside don't understand: *The hustle is built from pain just as much as its built from potential.*

A Way Out… and a Way In

Maybe you got into the game for the bread.

Rent was due.

Your mom was struggling.

Your kid needed diapers.

The jobs weren't calling you back—or when they did, they wanted to pay you minimum wage and maximum disrespect.

Or maybe you weren't broke, but you were invisible.

You wanted to matter.

You wanted your name to ring bells.

You wanted to control something—anything—in a world where you felt powerless.

So, you hustled.

Not because it was easy.

Not because it was glamorous.

But because—in that moment—it felt like the only path that let you *breathe*.

And to be honest, "the game" *did* teach you something:

- How to move with confidence.
- How to calculate risk.
- How to read people, make deals, navigate chaos.

- How to flip desperation, desolation, and despondency into *strategy*.

But here's the catch: *the same tools that helped you survive can eventually start destroying you.*

Because what begins as a way out often becomes a way in—into a lifestyle that won't let you go easy.

Because "the game" doesn't come with an off switch—it doesn't say, "That's enough, you've made it." It says, "One more move. One more flip. One more risk."

Until it's not just a job—it's your identity.

More Than Money, Less Than Peace

Most hustlers don't stop because they're tired—they stop because they hit a wall.

Maybe you caught a case.

Maybe you lost someone close.

Maybe you looked around one day and realized you'd stacked some bread, but hadn't built a life.

That's the thing nobody talks about: *The hustle can give you everything **but** peace.*

It can give you money, but not trust.

It can give you power, but not rest.

It can give you respect, but not love.

It can give you movement, but not direction.

You can have the whole city saying your name—but still feel like a stranger in your own skin.

You can have shoeboxes, suitcases, or even bags full of cash—but not one conversation that makes you feel understood.

You can be *surrounded* by people—but dying inside from loneliness, fear, and pressure.

The Unseen Toll

What you sacrifice for the hustle adds up over time. And what makes it dangerous is, "the game" rarely sends you a warning before it takes something from you.

- Your time.
- Your sanity.
- Your clarity.
- Your relationships.
- Your safety.
- Your purpose.
- Your sleep.

And if you're not careful, it'll take *you*.

That's the cold truth. And if that truth hits you in the chest right now, that's not shame—it's *awareness*. And awareness is the first step to being free to live the life you *want,* as opposed to living the life you *have* to.

And you don't have to hate "the game" to leave it behind—you can honor what it taught you, acknowledge what it gave you, and still choose something greater.

Because at some point, the question changes from "How do I get more?" to: **"What am I losing by staying in this?"**

THE SETUP FOR WHAT COMES NEXT

This book isn't about judging "the game"—it's about outgrowing it.

It's about realizing that survival isn't the same thing as living.

It's about turning "game" into guidance.

It's about shifting your energy from chasing the next move… to building a life that doesn't require constant escape plans.

Chapters 2 through 4 will dig deeper:

- What makes a hustler.
- Why we stay in this life even when we know it's killing us.
- And what it's really costing us—mentally, emotionally, spiritually.

Then we'll start the work of healing. Of transforming. Of building.

And this book ain't for everybody; it's for the ones who know there's more.

Who feel it in their gut.

Who are done with survival being their entire story, and actually want to *live*.

You've already proved you could make something out of nothing. Now prove you can make something that *lasts*.

> *Being a hustler doesn't make you broken –*
> *it makes you skilled. But when those skills aren't redirected,*
> *they become shackles and chains.*

Chapter 2

What Makes a Hustler?

You weren't born a hustler. You *were shaped and molded into one.*

Not by choice—but by circumstance.

Not because you wanted to take the hard way—but because the easy way didn't exist for people like you.

They don't hand out peace where you come from—they hand out *pressure*.

They don't hand out options—they hand out *obstacles*.

And if you somehow make it through, people call you "street smart" or "resilient"—but they don't see what it *costs* to be that sharp, that alert, that guarded, all the time.

Let's tell the truth: A hustler is not just someone chasing money! A hustler is someone trying to control what the world tried to take away!

The Anatomy of a Hustler

So, what makes a hustler, really?

Not just the grind—but the *wiring*.

Let's break it down:

Survivor's Mindset

A hustler learns early that no one's coming to save them. You had to grow up fast. You had to become your own backup plan. That means you learned to:

- Spot danger before it shows up.
- Think ten steps ahead.
- Pivot fast when plans fall through.
- Mask pain so it doesn't look like weakness.

True enough, survival taught you how to move in chaos, but here's the downside: *When peace finally shows up, it feels unfamiliar—even uncomfortable.* You're always waiting for the floor to drop out from under you.

Hyper-Responsibility

Most of the time, you took care of others before you took care of yourself. Maybe it was your siblings, your parents, your crew, your girl, your kids. *You* became the one people leaned on—even when your own back was *breaking*.

It made you strong, sure. But it also made you tired. And if you're honest, you probably don't even know what life looks like when it's *not* on your shoulders.

> *You were forced to grow up so early, you never had time to figure out who you really are.*

Emotional Armor

A hustler can't afford to be soft—that's what the world tells you. So, you build up armor: silence, sarcasm, suspicion, rage. Emotions become a liability.

But here's the truth: *just because you don't express the pain doesn't mean it isn't there.* It just hides. And when it hides too long, it rots—turning into outbursts, bad decisions, broken relationships, burnout.

Calculated Risk

You understand high stakes. You know how to make fast decisions. You see patterns others don't. That makes you dangerous—and valuable. But if that energy never gets redirected, it'll keep pulling you back into survival mode even when you don't need to be there anymore.

Not Every Hustle Looks the Same

Don't get it twisted—hustling isn't just selling dope or running scams. It can look like:

- Clocking three jobs just to pay the rent.
- Flipping kicks (sneakers), weed, cars, whatever moves.
- Managing your image so tight you can't breathe.
- Carrying everyone's emotional weight while acting like you're good.

Some people hustle legally. Some hustle emotionally. Some hustle spiritually. The point isn't *what* you do—it's the *state of urgency*, *exhaustion*, and *fear* you operate from every day.

That's what hustling really is: *living in permanent survival mode*.

> *You move fast. But you never feel still. You make moves. But you don't feel seen. You win. But you don't feel safe.*

That's the hustle nobody talks about.

Addicted to the Struggle

There's a point where hustling isn't just about making money anymore. It becomes your identity.

You don't know who you are without the grind.

You don't know how to rest without feeling lazy.

You don't know how to slow down without feeling exposed.

And here's the most dangerous part: *you start to confuse struggle with purpose*.

- You think chaos means you're important.
- You think stress means you're valuable.
- You think exhaustion means you're working hard enough.

That's the lie.

That's the trap.

That's the setup.

"The game" gave you motion, but it stole your direction.

You Don't Need to *Lose* Your Hustle— You Need to *Rewire* It

This book ain't about throwing away your drive—it's about *redirecting* it.

- The same mind that flipped work can flip a brand.
- The same energy that managed ten moving parts in "the streets" can manage a business.
- The same ability to read people can build networks instead of street alliances.
- The same resilience that kept you alive can now be used to *keep you well*.

You don't need to become a different person—you need to become a *more whole version* of the person you already are.

This chapter is about recognizing who you are—*before* the world told you to become something else to survive.

In Chapter 3, we'll talk about the things you've lost—or are still losing—by staying in survival mode:

- Time
- Peace
- Relationships
- Your sense of self

And if that sounds painful, good. Growth starts with truth. And you can't change what you won't face.

You've already proven you know how to survive.
*Let's find out if know how to **live.***

Chapter 3

The Hidden Costs of "the Game"

Every hustle has a price. But most people only count the money it makes—not the *life* it takes.

Nobody talks about the years lost in limbo. The people you pushed away to protect them—or protect yourself. The hours you spent chasing peace in chaos, only to realize you were never really at peace at all.

If you're reading this, you probably got out with your body intact. But what about your mind? Your heart? Your soul?

This chapter is about what "the game" really costs. Not just financially, not just legally. But emotionally, relationally, mentally, spiritually.

Because if we don't name the losses, we'll keep repeating them—generation after generation after generation.

The Time You'll Never Get Back

Hustling eats time. It eats days, months, years. You blink, and five years have passed—and all you've done is survive.

- Time spent on the block.
- Time spent ducking heat.
- Time spent plotting, running, rebuilding after every fall.
- Time spent in a kkkourtroom, jail, prison cell.

Even if you had money, you didn't have time.

- Time with your children? Gone.
- Time with your parents before they passed? Gone.

- Time when you could've been learning, healing, resting, building? Gone.

And here's the cold truth: *there is no refund on time*.

You can get money back. You can rebuild a reputation. But you can't buy back missed birthdays, holidays, quiet mornings, or peace of mind and moments of solace.

The game teaches you to move fast, but it never tells you what you're speeding past.

The People Who Paid with You

A lot of hustlers think they're carrying it alone. But no matter how "solo dolo" you think you move, other people feel the weight.

Your significant other loses sleep when you don't come home.

Your children lose innocence every time they sense your stress.

Your mother and father lose years off their lives from worrying about the knock at the door.

Relationships become transactions:

- You give money to make up for your absence.
- You give gifts to cover the guilt.
- You give silence instead of honesty because its "easier."

But people feel that... And slowly, they pull away. Or worse, they stay close—but never truly *with* you. Emotionally disconnected. Spiritually drained. Trust broken. Existing but not living.

Hustling may have fed your family – but did it nourish them?

The Self You Had to Bury

This is the part that hurts the most: the version of you that got left behind.

You weren't always like this. There was a time—maybe in childhood—when you dreamed, laughed easily, trusted people, believed in something better. But "the game" doesn't allow for that softness. So, you buried that self.

You became:

- Cold, so you wouldn't be hurt.
- Smart, so you wouldn't be fooled.
- Hard, so you wouldn't break.

But in the process, you stopped feeling. You stopped growing. You stopped imagining life outside of "the game."

And over time, you forgot who *you* were before survival became your personality.

This chapter is here to remind you: *that person is still inside you*. But they're waiting for the danger to end before they come back out.

The Illusion of Control

Here's a twisted part of "the game"—it makes you feel in control.

You run your own schedule.

You move how you want.

You don't answer to bosses, systems, rules.

But deep down, you know the truth: *You're not in control. You're reacting—constantly!*

Reacting to tension.

Reacting to threats.

Reacting to beef.

Reacting to the fear of being caught, set up, forgotten.

You're not free—you're *managing chaos*. And the more you convince yourself you're in charge, the more blind you become to how boxed-in you really are.

The game gave you power – but it took your peace.

The Loneliness That "Success" Can't Fix

Let's talk about that quiet feeling in your chest at night—when everything's "calm" but you still feel heavy.

That's loneliness. And money can't fill it.

You can buy booths and bottles at the club, cars, chains, validation—but none of it holds you when you're falling apart. None of it speaks truth when your spirit's spiraling. None of it knows the *real* you, the one behind the masks and moves.

Because here's the truth: When you've built your entire identity around being untouchable, nobody knows how to touch you.

So, you're surrounded—but isolated.

Loved—but not deeply known.

Respected—but not understood.

And you wonder why it still doesn't feel like enough.

Pain Isn't the Price of Purpose

You've lost enough. Time. People. Parts of yourself.

But here's the thing: loss isn't the end. It's the proof that something in you still wants more. It means something in you is still alive; still listening; still believing that peace, joy, love, freedom—they might actually be possible.

But first, you have to stop the bleeding. You have to stop pretending like you didn't lose anything. You have to look the cost in the face and say: *"I can't afford to keep paying this price!"*

SETTING UP CHAPTER 4

So now we've named what you've lost—in Chapter 4, we're going to name what you need to reclaim.

It starts with this hard truth: You can't hustle your way to healing.

You can't outwork pain.

You can't outrun the version of you that's wounded.

And you can't build a future while pretending the past didn't happen.

But healing is possible—and freedom is real.

In the next chapter, we'll talk about the inner shift that has to happen before the outer life can change.

It's time to stop counting losses—and start counting the cost of *not healing*.

Let's go there.

Chapter 4

You Can't Hustle Your Way to Healing

You can outrun the pigs.

You can outrun bills.

You can outrun "the streets," the beef, even your own failures.

But there's one thing no hustler has ever outrun: the pain.

It's always there.

Behind the drive.

Behind the grind.

Behind the silence.

And if you don't face it, it'll shape every decision you make—even the ones that look like success.

You can stack plenty of paper, drive the sweetest whip, throw money at any "problems" that come your way—even "retire" from "the game." But until you deal with what's underneath—the fear, the shame, the trauma, the grief—you'll still be trapped.

Hustling Is a Trauma Response

Let's say it plain: *hustling isn't just about ambition—it's about trauma.*

Not being seen.

Not being safe.

Not being supported.

Not being taught how to love, how to fail, how to feel.

When you grow up without stability, you learn to create control wherever you can. When you grow up around broken love, you learn to protect yourself with distance. When you grow up in chaos, silence and strategy become survival.

That becomes your hustle. Not just a job—but a shield. A wall. A weapon. A way to avoid pain.

> But here's the truth most hustlers avoid:
> You don't stop hurting just because you stop talking about it.

Pain Doesn't Disappear—It Multiplies

That breakup you never got over?

That loss you never cried about?

That rage you swallowed because there was no safe place to put it?

It's still in you.

And every time you bury one more feeling, one more truth, one more part of yourself… you lose a piece of your peace.

That pain becomes:

- Toxic relationships
- Self-sabotage
- Rage that explodes in the wrong moments
- Burnout you can't explain
- Numbness that no money can fix

And you wonder why nothing satisfies you. Why everything feels temporary. Why success feels just as heavy as struggle.

*Because pain unhealed doesn't disappear.
It just finds new ways to control you.*

Rest Isn't Weakness—It's Recovery

One of the hardest things for a hustler to do is *rest*. Not just sleep—but be *still*, emotionally, mentally, physically. To just be *still*.

Stillness feels unsafe: it feels like falling behind; it feels like weakness.

But the truth is: *rest* is when healing *happens*.

You can't reflect when you're always running.

You can't feel when you're always numbing.

You can't grow when you're always grinding.

But you don't have to live in *chaos* to feel *alive*.

And you don't have to *suffer* to be *strong*.

You can *choose* peace. But *only* if you believe you *deserve* it.

And that's the work: shifting from "I have to survive" to "I'm allowed to be well and thrive."

Letting Go of the Mask

To heal, you have to do something wild in hustling culture: *You have to tell the truth.*

Not to everybody—but to *yourself.*

You have to admit:

- "I'm *tired* of this bullshit."
- "I don't trust any-muthafuccin-body."
- "I've been pretending that I was cool with this shit for years."

- "I don't really know who I am without the grind."
- "I want more. But I don't know how to ask for it."

That truth?—that's the first crack in the armor. And in that crack, the light gets in.

This is where real transformation starts—not with money, but with *honesty*.

Because healing isn't about pretending you're okay. It's about finally being real enough to *become* okay.

Healing Doesn't Make You Soft—It Makes You Solid

Let's kill a myth right now: *Healing doesn't make you soft. It makes you dangerous in a new way.*

- A healed man can walk away from "disrespect" without feeling small.
- A healed woman can build a boundary without feeling guilty.
- And a healed hustler can look at "the game" and say, "I outgrew this"—and *mean* it.

Healing gives you clarity.

Healing gives you peace.

Healing gives you power—*real* power, the kind *no one* can take from you.

And once you taste it, you'll never trade it for the rush of survival ever again.

SETTING UP CHAPTERS 5-10

Now the real work begins.

- In Chapter 5, we'll talk about relationships—and why building families, love, or partnerships while you're still in survival mode is a recipe for collapse.
- In Chapter 6, we start to imagine life beyond the hustle—real exits, not just temporary pauses.
- In Chapters 7-10, we'll walk through new paths, mental shifts, financial literacy, emotional recovery, and spiritual growth.

This is the turning point; this is the pivot. You've faced the cost. You've named the pain. Now we shift toward a life that doesn't depend on survival, but on *wholeness*.

You can't hustle your way to healing.
*But you **can** heal your way out of "the game."*

Let's build that.

Chapter 5

Why Hustling Isn't Compatible with Relationships or Parenthood

Love requires presence.

Parenthood requires patience.

Partnership requires trust.

And "the game"?—it demands all three. And gives none back.

Let's just tell the truth:

You can't build a stable life with someone else while you're still living in instability.

You can't raise a child in peace when you're still at war with yourself.

You can't create emotional safety when you don't feel emotionally safe *inside your own skin.*

This isn't about being unworthy of love—it's about being honest about where you are. Because when you try to pour from an empty cup, all you do is spill hurt.

The Hustler's Love Dilemma

When you're hustling, your attention is divided. Even when you *want* to love right, you're in conflict with your own lifestyle:

- You're constantly looking over your shoulder.
- You're emotionally distant—not because you don't care, but because you can't afford to be vulnerable.

- You're guarding your schedule, your secrets, your movements—because trust is a luxury you haven't been able to afford.
- You're "in a relationship," but you're not *in* it—you're hovering, halfway, distracted by survival.

So even the best partner ends up feeling like they're competing with "the streets." And most of the time?—they are. In the world of hustling—whether it be street entrepreneurship, underground economies, or even high-risk legal grinds—one of the most overlooked costs is emotional: the challenge of sustaining a healthy, committed relationship. While "mainstream culture" often romanticizes the "ride or die" partner or the image of the hustler with a loyal love, the reality is far less stable. There's a fundamental tension between the life of a hustler and the demands of long-term, emotionally grounded partnership.

The Nature of "the Game"

To hustle is to survive in a system that may not be built for your success. It's about improvisation, speed, secrecy, and often volatility. The hustler's calendar isn't 9 to 5—it's 24 / 7. Loyalty is conditional, trust is fragile, and risks are everywhere. These conditions don't just challenge relationships—they often warp them.

However, real intimacy requires consistency, emotional availability, and long-term thinking. Hustling, on the other hand, demands adaptability, compartmentalization, and short-term gains. It's difficult—if not impossible—to maintain both at the same time. When you're constantly calculating your next move, it leaves little space to nurture another person's needs.

Survival Mode vs. Intimacy

Survival mode is the opposite of intimacy. Survival says:

- "Don't let them get too close."
- "Don't show weakness."
- "Don't trust too easy."
- "Protect the bag at all costs."

But intimacy requires:

- Vulnerability
- Patience
- Consistency
- Emotional availability

You see the problem? You're trying to build intimacy with a survival mindset. You're trying to love from a place that's still bleeding.

So, what happens?

- You push people away when they get too close.
- You sabotage the good ones before they can leave you.
- You confuse love with control, consistency with boredom, and peace with weakness.

And then you say, "Love ain't for me." Crazy, right?

But really?—you've just never had the *space* to love fully. The emotional freedom. The healed identity.

Love didn't fail you – hustling kept love from reaching you.

Trust and Transparency: A Dangerous Game

Committed relationships thrive on transparency. But in "the game," withholding information can be a survival skill. Whether you're hiding cash flows, legal risks, or associations with dangerous people, full honesty may not be safe—or even possible.

Imagine a hustler trying to explain to a significant other why they disappeared for two days, or why they can't disclose who they were with. Every omission chips away at intimacy. Eventually, suspicion replaces trust, and the emotional bond frays.

I lived this tension more times than I care to admit. There were nights when I walked back into the house, exhausted from handling things I couldn't talk about, and I'd see the doubt written all over my woman-at-the-time's face. She wanted answers, and all I could give her were half-truths or silence. To her, I looked like a man hiding something. But in reality, I was trying to protect her from a world that would swallow her whole if she ever got too close.

That's the paradox: the same silence meant to shield her only drove us further apart. I wasn't out "running game" on her or living a double life—I was simply surviving. But in her eyes, every gap in my story was another reason not to trust me. Love started to feel like an interrogation, and home stopped feeling like home.

The truth is, trust and secrecy can't coexist for long. If you open up, you put your freedom, even your life, at risk. If you keep quiet, you put your relationship at risk. Either way, something breaks. And when suspicion settles in, it's only a matter of time before love turns brittle and crumbles under the weight of all the words left unsaid.

Looking back, I realize this is one of the cruelest traps of "the game." It doesn't just test your loyalty in "the streets"—it tests your ability to be present, open, and whole in your most intimate relationships. In that sense, "the game" doesn't just take from you on the outside. It robs you of closeness, of family, of the very trust you need to make love last.

Therein lies the irony, right?—the very secrecy that keeps you alive in "the streets" is the same secrecy that poisons your home. To your significant other, what you call protection looks a lot like betrayal. Silence starts to feel louder than words, and distance grows where closeness once lived.

But here's the real danger—transparency in the wrong hands can be a death sentence. If your partner isn't built for the weight of that truth, if they share too much with friends, family, or even in a heated argument, your business can unravel. In "the game," loose lips don't just sink ships—they bury bodies.

So, what does a hustler do? Choose between survival and intimacy? Between safety and love? That's the impossible balance most never master. Some build relationships on half-truths and carefully chosen omissions, telling themselves it's for "protection." Others gamble by opening up fully, praying their partner is solid enough to keep their secrets locked. Both paths come with risks, and both often lead to heartbreak.

Furthermore—we have to realize that—trust, once broken, is almost impossible to rebuild. A hustler's significant other often begins to wonder: *What else aren't you telling me? Who else are you with? What danger am I in just by loving you?* That shadow of doubt changes the way they move, the way they look at you, the way they invest in the relationship. Eventually, what was once love becomes surveillance. What was once intimacy becomes interrogation.

And here's the hardest truth: in "the game," sometimes even your best intentions look like lies. You're not hiding things to cheat, but to "protect." You're not disappearing because you don't care, but because you're handling business. Yet intentions don't erase the loneliness your partner feels when you vanish, or the coldness of a bed that stays empty night after night after night.

In the end, trust and transparency are a dangerous game because they demand two things "the game" rarely allows: consistency and vulnerability. Without them, relationships collapse under suspicion—

and with them, you may not survive "the streets." And so, every hustler must face the same brutal question: *What are you willing to lose—your freedom, your life, or your love?*

The Illusion of Stability

Hustlers often appear confident and in control, but the reality beneath the surface is often chaotic. Financial highs come fast, but so do devastating lows. Committed relationships require some degree of predictability and planning—two things that are antithetical to hustling.

And—I can't reiterate this enough—bringing someone into your world when the foundation is built on sand isn't just unfair—it can be dangerous. For *both* parties.

The truth is, hustling breeds a rhythm of instability that outsiders rarely see. One day you're flush with cash, popping bottles and paying bills for everybody in your circle. The next day you're scrambling to cover a debt, avoiding calls, and calculating whether the walls are closing in. To the untrained eye, that kind of rollercoaster looks like adventure. To someone living it, it's survival on a tightrope with no safety net.

In relationships, instability doesn't stay "in the streets"—it seeps into the home. Missed dinners turn into broken promises. Unexpected disappearances start to look like betrayal. When your world runs on unpredictability, your significant other never knows if they're standing on solid ground, or if it's about to collapse beneath them. And after a while, that constant uncertainty erodes more than trust—it eats away at their sense of safety, too.

I've lived that illusion. There were nights I could make my woman-at-the-time feel like the world was hers, only to turn around and disappear into chaos I couldn't explain. I told myself I was shielding her from stress, protecting her from the darker truths of me being "out there in the streets." But what I was really doing was building her hopes on a foundation I knew might crack at any moment. That wasn't love. That was me asking her to carry the weight of my instability without giving her the tools—or the truth—to handle it...

The hustler's gift is adaptability, but in relationships, constant adaptation feels like whiplash. One day you're a giant in her life, the next you're a ghost. And while some partners try to ride the storm, most eventually realize they're drowning in someone else's chaos. That realization breaks more than relationships—it breaks the hustler, too. Because behind all the bravado, most of us crave the same thing we pretend not to need: a steady place to land, a sense of home.

The illusion of stability is seductive because it promises that you can have both—the adrenaline of "the game" and the comfort of love. But illusions fade, and when they do, you're left with either hard truth or heartbreak. The choice, ultimately, is whether to keep building on sand—or to step back and start laying something solid.

Emotional Labor and Burden

A committed partner to a hustler often bears emotional burdens they never anticipated—worrying about their safety, coping with erratic schedules, and being sidelined by "business." Love can't fix a lifestyle that is structurally opposed to emotional investment.

Many hustlers aim and claim to keep their personal and professional lives separate. But over time, the weight of both worlds tends to collide. The very traits that make someone effective in "the game"—emotional detachment, focus on self-preservation, hyper-independence—can become liabilities in a loving relationship.

What outsiders rarely see is how much quiet labor a significant other performs just to stay afloat beside a hustler. They become the ones steadying the home and children, covering for unexplained absences, masking worry when the phone rings late at night. They absorb the tension that comes from waiting on a knock at the door that could change everything. That invisible labor doesn't just weigh on your lover—it begins to distort the love itself. Instead of being nurtured, love becomes something carried, like a heavy bag that never gets set down.

I remember watching a woman I loved carry that weight without complaint, even though I knew it was crushing her. She did her best to be strong, did her best to trust the distance I kept between my worlds. But her eyes told the truth: she was tired of wondering if each day might be the one where it all came crashing down. I thought I was shielding her by not sharing details, by locking away parts of my life. In reality, I was asking her to fight a battle blindfolded, to love me without ever being given the full picture of what that cost.

The irony is that we hustlers often pride ourselves on independence—never needing help, never showing weakness. But that same independence forces our significant others to carry the emotional load alone. Every time I shut her out in the name of "protection," I was also shutting her deeper into loneliness. She wasn't my "partner in life" in those moments; she was my bystander, left on the sidelines of a "game" that threatened her peace even though she wasn't playing…

The cruelest truth is this: love can survive many storms, but it rarely survives being treated like a burden. Emotional labor is invisible until it becomes unbearable. And once it reaches that point, it's not just the relationship that breaks—the hustler, too, is left facing the emptiness of realizing that the very walls built to "protect" ended up pushing away the person they wanted most to keep safe.

A Case for Timing, Not Rejection

This chapter isn't arguing that hustlers are incapable of love or undeserving of commitment. It's a warning against prematurely seeking stability in a lifestyle built on *instability*. For some, love may need to wait until "the game" is over—or transformed into something more sustainable and honest.

That's a truth I learned the hard way. I used to convince myself that I could balance both: the grind that demanded secrecy and risk, and the kind of love that deserved openness and safety. But the two rarely coexist without one being sacrificed. When "the game" is in full motion, there's no pause button for romance. No matter how pure the intention, the lifestyle keeps pulling you back, making promises you can't keep and asking sacrifices you can't repay.

Realize, it's not rejection when a hustler steps back from love; it can actually be the deepest form of care. I've had to admit that in certain seasons of my life, I wasn't capable of being the man a particular woman needed me to be. I wasn't reliable enough, transparent enough, or free enough to let love grow roots. And rather than admit that out loud—or even to myself—I attempted stretching myself between two worlds. The result was heartbreak—for her *and* for me.

Real talk, timing is everything; what feels impossible in one season may blossom in another. Some hustlers do find love that endures, but often it's because they've either stepped away from the chaos or found a way to channel their ambition into something less destructive. Love needs ground that can hold its weight. Without it, no matter how deep the feelings, the foundation will crack.

Looking back, there's been a time or two where I wish I had realized it and been more honest about that. Instead of letting my woman-at-the-time feel unwanted or neglected, I could have explained that my war wasn't with her, but with myself and the life I was still entangled in. It wasn't that she wasn't enough—it was that I wasn't yet ready. That distinction matters, because rejection wounds, but truth can at least offer clarity and a chance for healing...

So, for anyone still in "the game," understand this: love may not be impossible, but it will demand timing, maturity, and transformation. To try to force it before those elements are in place are to risk breaking something—some*one*—beautiful. Sometimes the most loving thing you can do *is* wait—until you're ready to choose not just "the game" but the life beyond it.

Ultimately, it's about alignment. A committed relationship isn't just a title—it's a mutual agreement to build something real. And "the game," for all its allure and survival value, is often at odds with that vision. Until those paths can merge, the choice becomes clear: either change the lifestyle or delay the love.

> *You can love someone and still destroy them*
> *if you haven't done the work to heal.*

Why "the Game" Shouldn't Involve Parenthood—Yet

Let's talk about fatherhood (or motherhood). Because "the game" doesn't just test your ability to love—it tests your ability to show up.

You may provide; you may love your child more than anything. But if your hustle keeps you:

- Absent
- Emotionally shut down
- In danger
- In survival mode

… then your child is being raised in a world where love and instability come hand in hand.

And we both know how that ends—that's how *we* were raised. With love that hurt. With presence that felt like pressure. With role models who were strong—but not *safe*.

> *Providing is not parenting. Presence*
> *is not the same as **availability**.*

Children don't just need your money—they need your presence, your peace, your attention, your guidance. And you can't give what you've never had—or never healed.

Because parenthood is not a "game." It's not a symbol of success, a rite of passage, or something to check off a life list. It's a lifetime contract that demands stability, patience, consistency, long-term thinking, and your full unadulterated love. And for many hustlers, those are resources in short supply.

Understand that this chapter isn't about shame. It's about clarity. Because if you're still living in survival mode, chasing money through high-risk means, dodging legal trouble, or struggling to meet your own emotional needs, then having a child might be more harmful than healing—for both you *and* the child.

The Illusion of Providing

Let's get one thing out of the way: money doesn't make you a parent. Providing for a child isn't just about buying Jordans, designer clothes, or posting up with them on Instagram. It's about showing up—physically, emotionally, mentally, and spiritually—day after day after day.

Many hustlers scream, "I'm doing this for my kids." But if what you're doing might land you in prison or worse, what are you really providing? Children need presence more than presents. If your hustle puts your freedom, safety, or life at risk, it also puts your child's future in jeopardy. Can you dig it?

How do I know?—because I once believed the illusion myself. Time and time again I tried to sell myself the false idea that every "street dollar" I stacked was an investment in my children's future. And I foolishly thought that a pair of kicks, a tree full of gifts, or some new electronic toys would prove my love and care. Yet, when I was incarcerated and not there to help with the homework, to hear about the hard days at school or on the playground, or to just sit at the dinner table, those gifts I had provided were nothing more than band-aids on wounds I couldn't see. It was unfair to my children—and to their mothers whom I had left behind...

There's also the silent damage we don't like to admit. When a child watches a parent disappear for stretches at a time—locked up, hiding out, or too busy chasing the next move—they learn lessons we never intended to teach. They learn that money outranks presence. They learn that outsized risk is normal. They learn to normalize instability. And no matter how much we think we're shielding them from the realities of "the game," children see and feel more than we realize.

Understand: *real* providing is *consistency*. It's the parent whom shows up to school conferences, even if their kicks aren't the "latest." It's the one whom sacrifices the fast money for the long game of stability. It's the everyday grind of modeling patience, discipline, and resilience. These are the gifts that outlast any material thing, because they become part of whom the child is.

Realize that—maliciously—"the game" tricks us into thinking that financial provision can excuse emotional absence. Yet, if you're not *there* to guide your child through life, "the streets" will be waiting to do the job for you. And "the streets" don't provide—they consume. Real talk.

So, if I could speak to the younger me, the one whom thought every risky move was "for my kids," I'd tell that fool this: *Providing isn't about how much you give, but how often you're there. Shoes get old.* Memories don't. Children won't remember the price tags or the "name brands," but they'll never forget whether you were *present* in their lives—or absent.

The Trauma is Generational

Children are deeply sensitive to stress, instability, and chaos. They absorb it. If you're coming home on edge, always watching your back, disappearing for days, or bringing tension and danger into the household, your child will feel it—whether they understand it or not.

That trauma doesn't fade with age. It becomes a pattern. Many kids who grow up in that kind of uncertainty end up repeating it. If *your* life hasn't healed from what *you've* been through, why risk passing that cycle to the *next* generation?

Foolishly, I used to think that I could shield the people whom I loved from the more negative side of my choices; I thought that if I kept certain shit quiet—if I carried the weight myself—then they'd be safe. Yet, I didn't realize—at the time—that silence is heavy, too. And a child doesn't need the full story to sense that something is wrong; they pick up on the shift in your voice, the tension in your shoulders, the way the room feels "off" when you walk in. They feel the unspoken.

And when that becomes "normal," it adversely shapes them. A child growing up in an environment of uncertainty learns that love is unpredictable, that safety is temporary, that peace never lasts. They may not have the words for it, but the body remembers. The anxiety, the fear, the lack of trust—it sinks deep into their bones and psyche.

How do I know?—because, as with the illusion of providing, I carried that same weight from my *own* upbringing. I didn't want to admit it at the time, but part of the reason I was drawn to "the game" was because chaos already felt familiar. The risk, the highs and lows, the constant tension—it mirrored the instability I had witnessed and/or lived through myself. I mistook survival for strength. And in doing so, I unknowingly risked handing that same pattern down to the next generation…

That's the trap of generational trauma—it doesn't always look like abuse or neglect on the surface. Sometimes it looks like providing while stressed, loving while absent, protecting while still putting the family in danger. The cycle continues not because we don't care, but because we haven't healed. Because if we don't face our *own* scars, we end up passing them *forward*; *our* children will either repeat what they saw, or spend years unlearning that shit. Neither is fair to them.

Yet, breaking the cycle doesn't start with giving them more—it starts with giving them better. Better energy, better presence, better examples of how to navigate pain without letting it consume you. That's the real inheritance: teaching them stability in a world that often doesn't offer it…

Real talk—if we want our children to walk lighter than we did, then we have to do the work to put some of our *own* burdens down.

Time is a Currency Too

Hustling eats your time. You're always grinding, chasing, calculating. That's time you can't give back. I can't reiterate it enough: children require presence—not just being in the same room, but being emotionally available, patient, and consistent.

And if your mind is elsewhere—on the next flip, the next drop, the next escape plan—your child notices. You might be in the house, but not in their life. And one day, they'll feel the difference…

Foolishly, I used to think that if I made sure that my children "never wanted for anything," then all of the missed moments would somehow be balanced out. Birthdays I missed due to incarceration, school events I couldn't attend, dinners I left half-finished (when I *was* there!) because my phone rang—I convinced myself the payoff would be worth it. But the truth is, money doesn't rewind the clock. You can buy shoes, but you can't buy memories.

Because a child doesn't measure your love by what you put in their hand—they measure it by the moments you put in their heart. The small things add up: sitting on the floor helping with homework, listening to their stories, playing games with them—or even just laughing with them over nothing. Those are the investments that pay lifelong dividends. When you're absent, no matter how much you provide materially, what they remember most is the gap.

And here's the part many hustling cats overlook: your time spent isn't just valuable to your children—it's also valuable to *you*. Every moment *you* spend with them is a chance to ground yourself in something real, something that makes the risk and chaos of "the streets" feel smaller. "The game" takes and takes and takes, but *family* gives back—*if* you let it...

Understand: Children don't just want you to provide—they want you to participate in their lives. They won't remember how much bread you had in their childhood, but they will remember if you were there to share a sandwich. And if you weren't, the absence echoes...

So, recognize: time is a currency that doesn't replenish. Once it's spent, it's gone. The question every hustler has to ask themselves is: whom and what are you spending it on, and what will you have to show for it when the clock runs out?

Parenthood Without Peace Is a Setup

No child asks to be born. That means as parents, we have an obligation to create an environment where they can thrive. If your life is still rooted in chaos—whether that's "the streets," constant legal risks, or living in survival mode—then bringing a child into that environment is not only unfair, it's harmful.

Because children don't just live in our homes; they absorb our energy. They hear the tone of our voices; they notice the late nights; they sense the tension in the air. Even when you think you're protecting them from the truth, they're watching, listening, and learning. And what they learn in that environment becomes the foundation for how they see the world.

Furthermore, peace isn't only the absence of gunshots, arguments, or police sirens; peace means consistency. It means a child knows whom will be there when they wake up in the morning, and whom will tuck them in at night. It means not having to question if Moms or Pops will disappear suddenly—or if the home they're living in might be torn apart by the pigs or some "jackers."

Without peace, a child grows up in a state of constant alert. They learn to be anxious before they learn to feel safe. They learn secrecy before they learn trust. And often, they carry that survival mindset into their own adulthood, repeating the very cycles their parents thought they were protecting them from.

This is why parenthood requires more than money or material provisions. It requires an environment of emotional safety and nurturing. So, if you're still living in instability, the most loving decision might be to delay having children until you've built a foundation of peace. Otherwise, you're setting them up to inherit *your* battles instead of giving them the freedom to write their *own* story.

Understand: Children deserve more than clothing, shoes, shelter, and food—they deserve peace of mind. And peace isn't something you can fake. It has to be lived, created, and protected. Without it, parenthood becomes less about raising children and more about passing on unhealed wounds.

Ultimately, you may think you can shield your children from the world, but the truth is, they see more than you realize. They hear the tension in your voice, notice the lies, sense the fear. Yet, parenthood demands an environment where a child can grow without carrying the weight of adult survival. So, what are you going to do?

A Hard Pause, Not a Permanent No

Let me be clear: I'm not saying that you should never have children; all I'm saying is: "not yet." Not while you're still living in instability, surviving day to day, or caught up in the dangers of "the game." Children deserve to be raised in an environment where they can grow—not merely survive alongside you. Because parenthood works best when there is a foundation—structure, financial stability, emotional maturity, and peace of mind. That foundation doesn't have to be perfect, but it has to be steady. Children don't need a flawless parent; they need one whom is present, consistent, and safe.

So, the message here is simple: take a hard pause, not a permanent no. Build first, then bring life into that stability. Because when you *do* choose to bring a life into this world, they deserve a version of you that's ready. Not perfect—but *present*. Not rich—but *rooted*. Not hustling for survival—but building for legacy.

The Selflessness of Healing and Choosing Legacy Over "the Game"

Let's flip the script for a second: *Healing is a form of selfless love*. Can you dig it?

It's saying:

- "I'm not *going* to drag another person through my chaos."
- "I'm not *going* to put a child through the confusion I lived with."
- "I'm *going* to give my future family the version of me I never got growing up."

That's not weakness—that's maturity. That's legacy. That's real power.

*Hustling may make you a provider – but **healing** is what makes you a **protector**.*

A lot of us think we can build a family or a long-term relationship *while we're still figuring ourselves out*. And yes, some people grow together—but let's be honest: *most of us try to build before we've even healed.*

And when that happens?

- We create households full of unspoken trauma.
- We pass down emotional dysfunction as normal.

- We raise children who learn to *survive* love, not *receive* it.

Again, this book isn't saying "never love," or "never have children."

It's saying: Pause. Heal. *Prepare*. So, when you *do* love, when you *do* lead, you're doing if from a place of truth and not trauma.

At some point, every hustler has a choice to make: will I keep living for "the game," or will I start building a life beyond it? The truth is, "the game" demands too much to coexist with real love, family, and peace. It eats your time, drains your energy, and breeds chaos. And no matter how much you *think* you can separate "the streets" from your personal life, the two will *always* bleed together.

Never forget: serious relationships require trust, stability, and emotional availability—yet, "the game" thrives on secrecy, paranoia, and survival-mode living. And parenthood requires peace, patience, and consistent presence—however, "the game" steals all three. Furthermore, family demands sacrifice for something larger than yourself—while "the game" convinces you that the grind is sacrifice enough.

That's why this isn't about denying yourself love, partnership, or children forever; it's strictly about *timing*. "The game" may promise fast money and temporary validation, but family and legacy demand something altogether different. They demand structure, freedom, and peace of mind—and they demand healing. Until you've put "the game" behind you, you can't give those things fully to anyone else.

So, here's the challenge: don't confuse provision with presence. Don't confuse motion with progress. Don't confuse survival with legacy. Make the hard choice to pause. To heal. To build a foundation that isn't built on quicksand.

Because when you finally step away from "the game," you'll discover that the greatest move isn't stacking for yourself—it's creating a life where the people you love never have to feel the weight of "the streets" you once carried. That's when family, father/motherhood, and legacy become more than possible. They become attainable and sustainable. They become real.

Never overlook the fact that a true legacy isn't about how much you stack—it's about what you leave behind in the hearts and minds of your children and others. And that kind of legacy starts with discipline, patience, and timing. Hustling might feed you today, but parenting and lasting, loving relationships demand your forever. Don't make the mistake and mix the two until your world is ready to carry that weight.

Before you try to build a life with someone else, build one with **yourself**. *Before you chase* **legacy**, *learn to live without* **chaos**.

SETTING UP CHAPTER 6

So, what happens when you decide to stop hustling?

That's what Chapter 6 is about: *walking away from "the game"—and toward a life that doesn't revolve around survival.*

We'll talk about:

- The fear of letting go
- The loss of identity when you leave "the game"
- The discipline it takes to build new lanes
- And the courage to start over—for *real* this time

Because once you understand what love requires, what your peace costs, what your future deserves—"the game" starts to feel like a prison.

And this book?—it's the first set of keys.

Chapter 6

From Hustler to Legacy Builder—Life After "the Game"

So, you're ready to leave "the game" behind.

You feel it in your chest.

You've counted the cost.

You've seen what it's taken from you—your peace, your people, your purpose.

But now what?

How do you walk away from something that "raised" you? That fed you, clothed you, validated you? How do you say goodbye to a lifestyle that became your identity?

This chapter isn't just about quitting "the game"—it's about learning how to live without it. It's about confronting the fear, the emptiness, and the unknown that comes *after* the grind stops.

Because survival might be brutal—but it's familiar.

Peace on the other hand?

Peace is scary when you've never had it.

The Silence After the Noise

One of the first things you notice when you step away from "the game"… is the *silence*.

- No constant calls, pages, or pings.
- No rush to make a move.
- No paranoia.

- No chaos to distract you from yourself.

At first, that silence feels *wrong*—like something's missing. That's because "the game" didn't just fill your pockets—it filled your *nervous system*. You got addicted to the movement—the noise; the tension; the feeling of being needed, even if it was dangerous.

Now you're just... still. And for the first time, you have to *feel everything you've been running from.*

That's not a weakness—that's the beginning of healing.

Stillness is where the truth meets you.

You Are Not "the Game"

Here's the identity crisis that catches most people off guard: When you leave "the game," you don't just leave a lifestyle—*you leave a version of yourself behind.*

- The provider.
- The street savant.
- The one everybody called when they needed something.
- The one who was always in control.

Now... who *are* you?

This is where most people get stuck; they leave "the game" physically, but not *mentally*. They're still *thinking* like hustlers—still moving in fear; still needing validation through "moves."

So, they relapse. Not always back into crime—but into dysfunction. They find another form of hustle:

- Chasing clout online
- Bouncing from relationship to relationship
- Overworking themselves in "legit" spaces
- Numbing out with addictions or distractions

Because it feels *safer* than being still. Than rebuilding from scratch. Than starting slow.

But that slowness? That discomfort? That confusion? *That's the rebirth.* You're not broken—you're *becoming*.

Freedom Isn't Fast—It's Built

Let's kill the fantasy now: Leaving "the game" won't feel like a Netflix montage with dramatic music and instant success. It'll feel like:

- Confusion
- Boredom
- Doubt
- Shame
- Restlessness
- Jealousy watching others still "winning" in "the game"

But here's the difference: They're still *running* while you're finally *planting*.

You're learning how to:

- Budget
- Build
- Heal
- Trust
- Think long-term
- Sit with discomfort without blowing up your progress

This is *real* freedom. Not fast, not flashy—but *stable*.

And for cats raised on chaos, *stability is the scariest freedom of all.*

You're Allowed to Start Small

One reason people stay in "the game" is pride: You *were* someone; you had *respect*; you moved *heavy*.

Now you're folding clothes at a store, or driving Uber, or going back to school.

And your ego is screaming: *"This ain't me! This ain't who I am!"*

But listen closely: Your ego wants *applause* while your *spirit* wants *peace*.

There's absolutely no shame in starting small—there's only shame in staying stuck because you're too afraid to look "regular."

> *The real flex is building something that doesn't need to be hidden. Something your kids can visit. Something your heart can rest inside.*

So, don't be afraid to let the grind go.

Let the noise go.

Let the mask go.

Understand that there's life after "the game."

It's not louder.

But it's *truer*.

"The game" can teach you a lot—how to move smooth and smart, how to adapt, how to take risks and read people. Yet if that knowledge never evolves, it becomes a trap. The smartest hustlers aren't the ones still playing "the game" in their 40s. They're the ones who learned the rules, beat "the system," and then left the table to build something that lasts.

Because survival isn't enough anymore. It's time to shift from *hustling to live* to *living to build.*

"The Game" Has an Expiration Date

No one hustles forever—that's the first truth you have to accept. *"The streets" don't come with a pension plan.* They retire you in one of three ways: a casket, a cell, or a wake-up call you can't ignore. And when that day comes, the shine wears off quick. The bread stops flowing. The so-called loyalty disappears. And what you're left with is what you've built.

If you've built nothing—no skills, no stability, no legacy—you'll wake up at zero, right at the age when you should've been leveling up. I've seen cats who were once the loudest in the room reduced to silence, living off memories of what they "used to have." That's not living. That's surviving off ghosts.

The hard part is admitting the truth: "the game" was always temporary. It might feel eternal when you're on a roll, but the walls are always closing in. The real question becomes: *What do you want for yourself when it's over?* Fast money, or true freedom? Attention, or lasting impact?

Freedom means being able to move around without always looking over your shoulder. Impact means leaving something behind that speaks for you long after the applause is gone. Both require planning beyond the next flip. Both require discipline to shift from consuming to building.

"The game" has its season, but legacy has no expiration date. When "the game" ends, what will remain? That answer determines whether your story becomes another cautionary tale—or a blueprint for transformation.

You Already Have the Skillset—Now Redirect It

People underestimate hustlers. They look at our lifestyle and rightly see recklessness and danger, yet what they miss is the intelligence and skills that it takes to even *survive* in our world. Strategy. Salesmanship. Negotiation. Risk Tolerance. Vision. Creativity. These aren't just "street traits"—they're *entrepreneurial weapons*. Therefore—if you think about it—the problem isn't our *skillset*; the problem is the arena in which we've been *applying* it.

Consider this: to run a dope-spot / corner / block / trap-house, you're already managing supply, demand, and distribution, right? Moreover, to build a name and reputation, you have to market yourself *and* your product. Lastly, to navigate all of the danger out there, you're reading people, anticipating moves, and negotiating outcomes on the fly. That's just as much a business education as the one I earned in college—we just earned this education in "the streets." But that doesn't make it any less valid—or valuable.

But understand: the key for us is redirection. Applying those same instincts to real estate, entrepreneurship, investing, or even mentorship, the payoff isn't temporary like it is in "the streets"—in these turfs, it multiplies. And instead of constantly starting over after every loss, we start building equity, ownership, and reputation that grows with time.

Before my own "retirement," I had to realize that I didn't need to become *someone else*—I just needed to evolve into someone *more*. "The streets" had already taught me resilience, creativity, and the ability to adapt under pressure—those are transferable skills. And when we redirect them, we're not abandoning who we were—but instead transforming what we're capable of...

"The game" tricks us into thinking that it's the only stage where our gifts can shine; truth is, the same energy that kept you alive in chaos can build you a legacy in peace. And that's the real power: not changing your *essence*, but changing your *aim*.

Turning Respect into Influence

In "the game," respect is survival—your name carries weight because people know not to cross you, or because they admire how you move. But respect built on fear or fast money has a short shelf life; when the money fades or "the streets" shift, so does that respect. What lasts isn't how loud your name rang in the moment—it's the influence you leave behind.

Influence is legacy. It's when your presence continues to move people even in your absence. That's a different kind of power. Respect says, *"I see you."* Influence says, *"You changed me."* And that's the transition every hustler has to make if they want to outlive "the game."

Ask yourself: when it's all said and done, will people remember you as someone who just "got money," or as someone whom built something that mattered? Respect can make people listen, but influence makes people follow your example—or avoid your mistakes. Either way, it shapes the future beyond your immediate reach.

This is where building comes in. Whether it's a business that creates jobs, a program that gives youth an alternative to "hustling," or simply being the first in your family to break a destructive cycle—those moves echo louder than any street reputation. *Your name means something even when you're not in the room.* They speak on you not with fear, but with gratitude, with admiration, with hope.

I had to learn that real power isn't just loud, it's lasting. Anyone can demand respect in the moment, but influence lives on. And when your influence carries forward, your name doesn't just stay alive—it keeps working for you long after your hustle has ended.

Rewriting the Narrative

Too many hustlers never get the chance to rewrite their story; they get cut short—by prison, by violence, by betrayal. And once you're gone, you don't control the narrative anymore. People remember you for the wreckage or the reputation, not the potential. They talk about what you did, not what you could've become. That's the tragedy of "the game": it steals not just your time, but your voice in how your story is told.

However, if you're reading this, breathing right now—you still have a chance. The pen is in your hand. You can pivot. And the truth is, you don't owe an explanation to any muthafucca still stuck in the same cycle you're trying to escape. Growth always threatens the ones who refuse to move. That's not your burden to carry.

Understand, too, though, that walking away from "the game" doesn't erase your past, nor does it make you less "real." If anything, it shows you had the courage and clarity to see past the illusion. Because being "real" isn't about dying for nothing—it's about living for something greater.

Rewriting the narrative means reclaiming your story before someone else writes the ending for you. It means flipping the script from "just another hustler who crapped out" to "the one whom broke the cycle." From "fast money" to "lasting legacy." From "fear and survival" to "freedom and impact."

That shift isn't about denying where you've been—it's about showing that where you've been isn't the only place you belong. "The game" will tell you there's only one ending, but that's the biggest lie it sells. The truth is: you *can* walk away, and when you do, you prove to everyone watching that another ending is possible.

You story doesn't end with "the game" unless you let it. Rewriting the narrative is how you make sure your name stands for more than what you risked—it stands for what you built.

What Legacy Really Means

Legacy isn't just about what people say after you're gone—it's about *what you build and protect while you're here.* Too many hustlers confuse legacy with reputation, but those aren't the same thing. Reputation is loud—it's about how many people know your name. Legacy is quiet—it's about how many lives your name changed.

Legacy is the children you raise or mentor. It's the business you create that outlives you. It's the people you lift when they're stuck in the same place you once were. It's the peace you protect for your family so they don't inherit the chaos you endured. Legacy is less about ego and more about impact.

When I think about legacy now, I don't picture flashy moments; I picture stability: my loved ones knowing they're safe, my name carrying weight because it opened doors, not because it closed coffins. That's a shift in values—from *proving* yourself to others to *preparing* something for others. Can you dig it?

And here's the real truth: quiet money, quiet growth, and quiet power are often the most unshakable kinds. The noise of "the game" fades, but what you've built in silence—assets, wisdom, relationships—becomes unmovable. That's why real legacy builders don't chase attention—they chase *roots*. They focus less on being remembered for the moment and more on leaving something that lasts beyond it.

Understand that your legacy is written in every choice you make: do you take from your people, or do you give back to them? Do you leave them with scars, or do you leave them with strength? That's the measure that matters. Because at the end of "the game," nobody will care about how fast you "got money"—they'll care about what you left standing when the bread was gone.

The Next Chapter Is Yours to Write

"The game" was never meant to be your whole book—it was just an opening chapter. For some, it was a test of survival; for others, it was a school of hard lessons. Nonetheless, it was never supposed to be the end of your story. And the danger is when cats mistake the first few pages for the entire narrative.

Now it's time to write the rest—with intention, structure, and purpose. That means shifting from reaction to creation, from chasing survival to designing a future. You've already proven you can navigate chaos; you've endured nights when the odds were against you and mornings when you didn't know if you'd make it back. That takes grit. But grit alone isn't enough. Now it's about direction…

The beauty of life after "the game" is that the pen is in *your* hand—nobody else gets to dictate the ending unless *you* hand it over. *You* can decide whether your name gets tied to temporary respect or lasting influence. *You* can decide whether your children inherit cycles of struggle or foundations of peace and love…

Writing the next chapter of your story doesn't mean forgetting the old one: it means honoring the lessons while refusing to be defined by the losses. It means proving that survival was just the first step—and that true strength is in building something that outlives the chaos.

So, the challenge is this: use the same drive that kept you alive to now create something that keeps you free. Channel the same vision you had for your hustle into a vision for your legacy. Prove to *yourself—and* to *everyone watching*—that the most powerful story isn't how you played "the game," but how you walked away from it and built something greater.

Because your story isn't finished - and the next chapter is *yours* to write. And if *you* choose, it can be the one that finally changes everything…

SETTING UP THE NEW BLUEPRINT

The next chapters are where we build that life:

- In Chapter 7, we'll dig into financial literacy—so you can stop chasing fast money and start building real wealth.
- In Chapter 8, we'll talk mental and emotional health—the therapy, self-reflection, and habits that help you stay grounded.
- Chapter 9 is about legacy—redefining success in your community, becoming a mentor, and giving back in real ways.
- And Chapter 10 is about faith, spirituality, and identity—because healing ain't just about what you stop doing; it's about who you *become*.

This is where we pivot—not from hustler to civilian, but from survivor to *builder*.

You've already proven you can hustle; now prove you can *heal*.

Chapter 7

Exit Strategies, Financial Literacy & Long-Term Wealth for Former Hustlers

Let's be real: You know how to get money—but do you know how to *keep* it? How to *grow* it? How to make it work while you *rest*?

"The game" taught you how to make money and move fast, how to flip, how to stretch and "flex"—but not how to *keep* your bread, grow it, or heal the part of us that only feels valuable when we're holding stacks. Nor did "the game" teach you how to build legacy; it taught *survival*—not sustainability. That's the trap. Because without a wealth mindset—without emotional clarity and discipline—we'll forever end up broke, even when our pockets are full.

This chapter is about a different kind of hustle: one rooted in longevity, not urgency. One that rebuilds the bag *and* the soul. It's about reclaiming your power—not by grinding harder, but by *getting smarter*. Because money that's earned but never *understood* is just money waiting to leave you.

And look—you already understand the core concept: The whole "game" is about what brings money *in* and what takes money *out*. That's it. That's the whole financial universe right there. Everything else is just details:

Fast Money vs. Free Money:
Fast Money Has No Foundation

Let's start here: *Fast money feels good. Free money feels better.*

Fast money is:

- High risk
- High stress
- High maintenance
- Emotionally taxing
- Legally dangerous

You're always one mistake, one raid, one betrayal away from losing everything.

Free money is:

- Slow at first
- Low stress
- Backed by structure
- Growing while you sleep
- Peaceful in your pocket

"The streets" pay, but they don't teach. They don't give us credit scores, equity, or tax strategy. Free money is what investments give you; what credit makes possible; what assets build. And most importantly: *what peace of mind protects.*

We may have earned thousands, even millions—but how much did we invest? How much did we *keep???*

Because no matter how good the run was, if we didn't grow it, we bullshitted and all we did was feed a cycle that dies as soon as we stop "moving around."

Here's the truth:

Fast money feels good because it fills a void! But that high comes with burnout, paranoia, and self-neglect. Real wealth doesn't come with fear—it comes with *freedom*. You've earned enough to know what money can't fix; now it's time to learn what money can do—when it's managed with wisdom.

What "the Streets" Don't Teach You About Money

You don't need a finance degree from a fancy college—all you need is a new mindset and a basic toolkit. Starting simple, here's what most hustlers never learn—because "the game" doesn't reward long-term thinking:

Cash Flow Isn't the Same as Wealth

So, listen; this is a critical distinction that keeps a lot of cats stuck in a trap—even after they get a little money: *Cash flow is the water you drink today, while wealth is the well you own that gives you water for life.* Can you dig it?

You can have a $1,000,000 in the shoe box and still be broke if you don't own anything of substance. Wealth isn't about what you make (your income)—it's about what you *keep* and what *grows without you.*

Cash flow is that money hitting your hand *right now*. It's the paycheck, the profits from a flip, the rent from a tenant. It's immediate. It feels good. It's what you use to pay bills, buy food, and survive. But here's the problem: the second you stop moving, the cash flow stops. No work? No pay. No hustle? No income. It's active. It keeps you on the treadmill.

Wealth is different. Wealth is silent. It ain't about what's in your pocket today; it's about what you own that pays you whether you're working, sleeping, eating, shitting, or on vacation doing a combination of all of the above. Wealth is the assets—the rental properties, the businesses, the stocks—that generate that cash flow *for* you, automatically.

Think of it like this: A king who just collects taxes is living off cash flow. But the king who *owns the land* the taxes come from? That's wealth. The land is the asset. It has value itself and it produces income.

A hustler with a fat stack from a "nice lick" has cash flow. It looks like wealth, but it's fragile. He blows through it on liabilities—whips, chains, rent—and soon he's back on the prowl looking for another "lick" to hit. But the cat whom used that same cheddar to buy a duplex?—now he has a tenant paying his mortgage. That duplex *is* wealth. It appreciates in value over time and it spits out cash flow every month, long after the original bread is gone.

Cash flow feeds you today—wealth feeds your bloodline for *generations*. Don't confuse the meal for the means to cook forever.

Income Without Structure Is a Setup

This is one of the most important lessons you'll ever get: You think the goal is just to get money, but that's only half the battle. The *real* goal is to *keep* it and make it work for you. And that's where structure comes in.

Because income without structure is like water in your hands: No matter how much you catch, it's going to leak through your fingers until you're left with nothing but wet palms. You might have a nice bankroll today, but without a plan, it's already on its way to being gone.

Here's why that fast, unstructured money is a liability in disguise:

- **It Tricks You Into a Lifestyle You Can't Afford:** That "big lick" hits having you feel like you made it, so you upgrade everything: the car, the apartment, the jewelry, the parties. You start living like your *current income* is guaranteed forever. But in "the streets," ain't shit guaranteed. That bread is a flash flood, not a steady river. And when it dries up—and it *always* dries up—you're left with a bunch of monthly bills you can't pay. That's how a blessing becomes a curse. You're not rich; you're just renting a lifestyle for a little while.

- **It Attracts Leeches, Not Partners:** When you're flashing with no foundation, you don't attract builders; you attract consumers. Everybody wants a piece of the come-up. They see you eating and come to get a plate. But no one's talking about how to help you plant a garden so you can eat for life. The money draws attention, but the wrong kind. It makes you a target, not a titan.

- **It Forces You Back to the Trap:** This is the biggest set-up. You have no safety net. No investments working for you while you sleep. So, when that unstructured income runs out—and, again, it will—your only option is to go right back to the same risky hustle to get more. It's a cycle. You're not building an exit strategy; you're just funding the same dangerous loop. You're a hamster on a wheel, running faster and faster just to stay in the same damn place.

Structure is the blueprint. It's what turns that water into a pipeline. It's: A budget. An emergency fund. Investments. Legal entities. Without structure, you're not really balling—you're just a temporary holder of cash on its way to someone else's pocket. Income without structure isn't freedom; it's just a longer chain.

You Can't Out-Earn Financial Illiteracy

It doesn't matter how much you make. If you don't know how to manage it, you'll always stay in survival mode.

> *"The game" gave you income. Financial literacy gives you freedom.*

This is the ultimate truth that "the streets" doesn't teach you, but you can't outrun this one; it's a mathematical law, like gravity. You might be able to jump higher than most, but gravity *always* wins.

Think of it like this: Financial illiteracy is a hole in your pocket. A hole in your boat. A hole in your bucket.

It doesn't matter how much water you pour into a bucket with a hole in it—it'll never really get full. You can have a firehose of income—a million-dollar rap deal, a "sweet lick" or flip, a massive inheritance—but if the bucket is leaking faster than you can fill it, you will *always* end up with an empty bucket. Always.

Here's why it's impossible to win this race:

- **The Temptation to "Lifestyle Up" is Too Strong:** When a huge chunk of change hits your hands with no plan, the first and only thing you know how to do is *spend*. You buy the status symbols you were denied: the luxury whip (leased), the jewelry (depreciating asset / borderline liability), the designer everything (liabilities). You're not building wealth; you're just *transferring your money to someone else's wealth*. You're making the car dealer, the jeweler, and the landlord richer. Your increased income just finances a more expensive version of being broke.

- **You Don't Know What to *Do* with the Money:** You know how to get it, but not how to keep it so it just... sits there. In a shoe box. Buried in your Mama's backyard. Or even in a checking account. Or worse, it burns a hole in your pocket. You don't know anything about: asset allocation—what to buy that'll grow; tax strategy—how to keep the government from taking a huge bite; liability management—how to avoid debt that eats you alive with interest. Without this knowledge, money is just a temporary visitor. It has no home, no purpose, so it leaves.

- **You Become a Target:** Big money + no financial IQ = a walking ATM. You attract "friends," "managers," "advisors," and "family" with their hands out. You get hit with bad investment deals, scams, and guilt trips. You can't say no because you don't have the literacy to see the scam or the confidence to protect your capital. Your bread gets siphoned off until it's gone.

- **There's No Safety Net:** When every dollar is spent on the *image* of wealth, there's nothing left for the *reality* of life. A lawsuit, a medical emergency, a dry spell in work, a court case—any unexpected crisis becomes a catastrophe. You're forced to go into high-interest debt or liquidate what little you have at a loss. The higher your income was, the harder and faster you fall.

The bottom line: Financial literacy isn't about pinching pennies—it's about building a system. It's the blueprint for the bucket. It patches the holes and tells the water where to go—into investments, into assets, into generational wealth. Understand, a cat with a $50,000 salary and a financial plan is wealthier than a fool with a $500,000 check and no clue. The first cat is building—while that second fool is just waiting to lose. You can't outrun a leaky bucket; the only solution is to *fix* the bucket.

---

*Maybe your parents never taught you how to manage money – but they did teach you survival. Now it's on **you** to evolve survival into structure.*

Ownership Over Flex: Assets vs. Liabilities

So, let's break it down—because you've heard me mention these terms a time, or two: assets vs. liabilities. And fucc Webster's or Oxford's dictionaries!—I'm going to give it to you in a language in which you already understand:

An "asset"?—that's your "Worker." An asset is something that *wakes up every single morning and goes to work for **you**!* It puts money *in* your pocket. True enough, you might have to set it up and you may have to look after it, but once it's pushing?—it's on the payroll, earning it's keep and then some.

Think of it like this: That pack you flipped—turning $500 into $1,500—that pack was your *asset*; it worked for you. Even the cats in the trap whom you had clocking for you?—they were your *assets* in a twisted, fuccd-up kind of way. They generated *income* for you.

But in the "legal" world, assets look different; they're not about tearing the community down, but instead building it—and *you!*—up all at the same time.

Real world assets—the legal kind:

- **A rental property:** That house you own? The tenant pays you rent every month. That mortgage payment comes out, but the rent check coming in is bigger. That property is your worker, on duty 24 / 7.

- **A business:** A barbershop, a laundromat, a detail shop, etc. People come in, pay for a service, and that cash goes into the register. After you pay the bills and your workers, the rest is profit. That business is your squad, generating legal revenue.

- **Stocks & investments**: You buy a piece of a company like Apple or Nike. Every time some fool buys a new iPhone or a pair of Air Forces, the company makes money, and because you own a piece, (every little now and again) they cut you a little check (called a dividend). Your money is out there on the street, hustling for you, and you don't even have to leave the house.

- **Yourself (Skills):** "The game" taught you how to manage people and "situations," negotiate, handle pressure, and spot opportunities—those are *skills*. Enhance them, use them, *add* to them. Say, for instance, if you get certified in a trade—like being an electrician, a plumber, a HVAC technician—those skills are assets. People pay you to use them. Those skills are your number one soldiers. And they can never be taken away from you.

Now as for "liabilities,"—*those are anything that reaches into your pocket and takes bread out without reimbursing it and* **then** *some!* Liabilities *drain* you; they're anything or anyone that eats your money without offering anything of appreciating value in return. Those shits are some leeches. The particular liability might look fly, it might feel good, but it's a leak in your boat. And, of course, if you have too many leaks, you sink. Simple as that.

Think of it like this: That fiend that always owes you money?—a liability. Who knows if they'll ever pay you back or decide to one day snitch you out or set you up in some other kind of way? Same thing for that flashy ass car you rented for the weekend to look like you "had it"—it took bread out your pocket just for "the experience"—and also probably ran you hot and put you on the radar of the "Alphabet Boys," scheming ass cats and kittens, and even robbers.

Real world liabilities—the legal kind:

- **A car note (on a depreciating car):** You copped a new Charger off the lot with a $800/month payment. The second you drive it off the lot, it's worth thousands less. And every month, that payment comes out of your account. It's not *making* you money—it's *costing* you money. And, furthermore, that car is a snitch—feeding information about your finances straight to the bank and the feds.
- **Designer clothes & jewelry:** You drop 10 racks on a bullshit chain. The moment you walk out the store, you'd be lucky to get half of that back if you had to sell it. That shit is dead money—a liability, a loss. It's not working for you; it just *cost* you.

- **Rent on a house you live in:** Now, this is a tricky one—because you do need a place to live, so it's a necessary cost. But the only way your spot is an asset instead of a *liability*, is if you're *purchasing* the home and it's *appreciating* (growing!) in value instead of *depreciating* (decreasing!).

- **Credit card debt:** Straight up, this is the worst kind of liability, in my opinion. You essentially bought air with this shit. You bought a "moment." And now you're paying 25 % interest on it. That's a fiend that will never, ever stop knocking on your door. The only recommended use of credit cards—in order to build or rebuild your credit—is paying a bill that you would have to pay anyway, and then *pay your credit card off completely before you owe even one cent in interest*. Other than that, stay clear of that bullshit.

Buying liabilities (cars, designer, jewelry) might get you applause from certain "elements," but buying *assets* (property, stocks, businesses) gets you peace and prosperity. Quiet money moves better than loud ego. Because the goal of "the game" has always been the same, right?—get more money—yet "the streets" will have your mind twisted thinking that jewelry and rented whips are assets because they bring you attention and "clout." But none of that shit translates to cash in hand, so understand those as "liabilities"—draining the very resources you may have risked your life to get.

Smart "game" is this: Use the vast majority of your cheddar to *buy assets*, and *then* let a (small!) percentage of the income *from* those assets to pay for your liabilities and lifestyle.

Stop being the asset for someone else.

Stop making the car dealership rich.

Stop making it easier for the jewelry store owner's ugly ass children to be able to attend college *debt-free* while *yours* have to scramble for scholarships, grants, and/or take out loans.

Real talk. Build your army of assets and put their asses to *work* for you and become a real general.

So, the next time you get some money, ask yourself one question: Am I going to make this bread work for me, or am I just going to keep having to work to make some more bread? The answer will tell you everything you need to know about your future.

Wealth Without Healing Is Just a Fancier Cage

Now let's be clear: *making money is only half the equation.* If we don't address the emotional wounds and beliefs behind our spending habits, wealth will slip through our hands time and time again.

- If you're buying things to feel seen, ask yourself why you feel invisible.
- If you sabotage your success, ask what "being stable" triggers inside you.
- If you're addicted to chaos, maybe peace still feels unsafe.

This is where therapy, journaling, spiritual work, or even deep conversations with yourself come in. Financial trauma is real—and it's often passed down through generations.

When you manage your money, you manage your *life*. You protect your time. You buy back freedom. You invest in rest. You leave behind something your children can build from—not just recover from.

Let your healing and hustle mentality work together:

- Go to therapy *and* build a business.
- Unpack your triggers *and* your taxes.
- Forgive your past *and* secure your future.

Become as "whole" as possible. Primarily for yourself—but also for those around you. Let's be clear: *Money won't fix your trauma.* But it *can* pay for therapy. It *can* buy time to rest. It *can* allow you to make *values-based choices, not desperation-based ones*. That's the difference between money as a trap and money as a tool. And when you finally treat money as a *servant*, not a god—you'll stop losing your peace to get it.

Breaking Emotional Generational Curses

You can be the first in your bloodline to:

- Own a home.
- Start a trust for your children.
- Retire without stress.
- Have money in the bank *and* peace in your spirit.

But that starts with healing:

- Stop normalizing burnout.
- Stop glamorizing poverty with pride.
- Stop repeating the belief that being broke is noble and being rich is evil.

Our ancestors survived for us to *thrive*—not just to repeat the struggle in cleaner clothes. The real bag is peace of mind. Generational stability. The freedom to choose how you live instead of letting life choose *for* you. The real "flex" is healing your habits and building your wealth at the same time.

Let "the streets" teach you grit, but let your healing teach you *growth*.

Because the goal isn't just to get out of "the game"—it's to never have to look back.

The Wealth Tools You Were Never Taught

Budgeting Is Strategy, Not Scarcity

Not just for broke people, budgeting is the blueprint for wealth—not a punishment. It tells your money where to go before it gets spent (and keeps you, then later, from wondering where it went!). It's power through preparation. Whether you make $500 or $5,000 a week, *every dollar needs a job!* Start simple:

- Needs
- Wants
- Savings
- Investments

Apps like EveryDollar, YNAB, Mint, and Wallet by Budget Bakers can help.

Credit Is Leverage

If cash is king, credit is the kingdom. Learn your credit score, fix your report, and use credit cards to build—not bury—your future. Debt isn't the enemy in the "real world" like it is in "the streets"—*undisciplined spending* is!

And your street reputation doesn't translate to the financial system. But your credit score?—that's how banks and even some businesses decide if they can trust you. So:

- Pay your bills on time
- Keep your balances low
- Use secured cards to rebuild if needed
- Monitor regularly (Credit Karma, Experian)

Because credit can open doors to:

- Business funding
- Home ownership

- Lower rates on loans

Savings & Emergency Funds = Survival Kit

You never know when life hits—but peace of mind is the best investment you'll ever make. Although "the game" foolishly trains you to spend now because you don't trust the future, that's a consumerist attitude. However, *healing* teaches you to save—because you're *investing in your future self and the lives of those whom you love.* That's the wealthy attitude of a *legacy* builder.

Start with:

- $500 - $5,000 for emergencies such as car repairs, hospital co-pays, etc. in a no-penalty CD (certificate of deposit)
- An additional 6—12 months of expenses in a high-yield savings account
- Auto-deposit to savings a small % from every check or deposit you earn

Investing

Investing is how wealthy people stay wealthy—they *make their money work* while they rest. Start with what you know, of course—e-commerce, real estate, service businesses—and then go from there. And, for sure, don't chase hype—learn that shit before risking a bus token. Read. Watch tutorials. Take free courses. Flip intellect the same way you flipped product.

Also, learn the basics of direct cash investing:

- Index funds
- Roth IRAs
- (REITs) Real estate investment trusts
- Dividend-paying stocks
- Treasury bonds & bills

And be wise enough to start small. $100—$1,000 monthly is a seed. Let it grow.

Business Structuring

You were already a CEO. Just in the wrong game. Time to step it up. Accordingly:

- Register an LLC
- Separate business / personal accounts
- Pay quarterly taxes
- Build a brand, not a hustle

And if you don't know how? Again, *ask. Learn. YouTube it. Pay* someone. That's how wealth gets built—through structure.

New Goals, New Game

Forget "get rich quick." Let's try this instead:

- Be *quietly* financially free.
- Buy back your time.
- Leave something for your children that's legal, clean, and growing.
- Give back to your community from overflow, not exhaustion.
- Learn to enjoy wealth without needing to *prove* it.
- This is the part they never taught us in the streets:

It's not about how much you make
*– it's about how well you **live.***

Getting out of "the game" doesn't mean walking away from everything and everyone you know. It just means repurposing your skills and experiences to build something real—something that pays you back without putting your life or freedom on the line. For many, that starts with three proven paths: entrepreneurship, creative outlets, and mentorship.

These aren't fantasies or "Plan Bs." They're real strategies that can turn your grind into growth. But each one requires a shift—not just in how you move, but how you *think*.

Entrepreneurship—From Street CEO to Legit Boss

Let's be real: most hustlers already run a business. It may not be registered, taxed, or advertised, but it has supply chains, marketing, customer service, risk management, and profit margins. That means you already have *entrepreneurial DNA*—now it's time to make it legal and scalable.

What it looks like:
- Flipping houses instead of flipping product.
- Running a clothing line instead of reselling streetwear.
- Opening a food truck, detailing shop, or mobile barbershop.
- Launching a service business—cleaning, logistics, landscaping, appliance and/or electronics repair.

Why it works:
You control the pace, the vision, and the branding. Plus, the satisfaction of creating something with your name on it hits different. No middleman. No hiding. Just growth you can build and pass down.

What it takes:
Discipline. A basic understanding of finance and marketing (which you can learn free online). And the willingness to *start small and stay consistent*.

You don't need a business loan or huge following.
You need a product, a plan, and patience.

Creative Outlets—Turning Pain into Power

The most profound art often comes from real struggle. Music, film, poetry, fashion, photography—these are more than hobbies. They're industries. And for many who come from "the game," they're lifelines.

Whether you rap, paint, design, shoot videos, or write—it can be a way to process your experience, tell your story, and monetize your truth.

Why it works:

Art gives pain a purpose. It turns isolation into connection. And in an era where authenticity sells, your voice can cut through the noise if you know how to use it.

Examples:

- Self-publish an e-book or memoir about your life.
- Start a podcast about street culture and real-life redemption.
- Sell prints, beats, or short films online.
- Partner with a local gallery or community center.

Your story isn't a weakness – it's a weapon! Use it with precision!

Mentorship—Be the Person *You* Needed

One of the most powerful transformations is going from hustler to healer. You know "the system." You know "the streets." You know the costs. That makes you valuable—not just to your peers, but to the next generation.

Mentorship isn't about being perfect; it's about showing up, being real, and offering guidance before someone makes the same mistakes you did.

What it looks like:
- Speaking at schools or juvenile centers.
- Starting a youth program or afterschool initiative.
- Partnering with reentry programs or nonprofits.
- Informally mentoring younger people in your neighborhood.

Why it works:
You become a mirror that reflects possibility. You interrupt cycles. And at the same time, you heal parts of yourself by helping someone else make a better choice.

> *Mentorship isn't charity – it's legacy. And you're qualified the moment you choose honesty over ego.*

We'll touch more on this in Chapter 9.

Choosing the Right Path for You

Not every road will feel natural at first. But pick the one that makes you feel *invested*, not just involved. Something that gives you a reason to wake up every morning without watching your back.

Start where you are. *Use* what you know. *Learn* what you don't.

And remember that there's no shame in starting small—there's only regret in not starting at all!

Each of these paths offers more than just income; they offer *healing through action*. Entrepreneurship teaches ownership. Creativity helps you process pain. Mentorship lets you repair the past by protecting the future.

This is how you hustle for your soul—not just your pockets.

"The game" didn't make you—but what you build after it *will*!

SETTING UP CHAPTER 8

Now that you've got the financial tools... Let's talk about the emotional foundation to protect them. Because what good is wealth if your anxiety still owns you? What good is stability if you still sabotage it?

In Chapter 8, we dig into mental wellness, emotional recovery, and breaking generational patterns - this is where you stop just surviving the trauma that raised you and start healing it.

Your bank account might be growing; now it's time to grow your *peace*.

Chapter 8

The Mask We Wear—Mental Wellness, Emotional Recovery, and the Inner Work of Breaking Generational Curses

Let's get to it: Most of us didn't grow up with therapy—we grew up with silence. With toughness. With "don't cry." With "man up." With "get over it." With "life's hard."

So, we never learned how to process pain—we just learned how to perform through it.

And the hustle?—that's a performance. It's loud, but it's hiding something.

Because behind every hustler is a kid whom got hurt. Whom got neglected. Whom saw too much, too early. Whom had to be "the man" before he knew how to be human.

And you can run the streets all you want—but at the end of the night, when the room's quiet and you're alone with yourself? *That kid is still in there.* Still waiting on you to come back and *heal* him.

In "the game," we're taught to move like nothing touches us. No fear. No emotion. No weakness. Keep our circle small, our guard high, and our pain buried deep. It's survival—but it comes at a cost: *we forget how to feel anything real.*

Relationships suffer. Community ties fray. And worst of all, our mental health—our sanity—gets left bleeding in the dark. In a culture that praises toughness, we never talk about the trauma we carry or the emotional numbness we mistake for strength.

It's time to start talking and let that shit out.

The Shit We Carry

Let's stop pretending—most of us are carrying:

- Unprocessed grief
- Rage we can't explain
- Trust issues that ruin every relationship
- Shame we never talk about
- Guilt from things we did to survive
- Self-hate dressed up as confidence
- A fear of failure so deep, we stay grinding just to avoid silence

You're not just tired because you work hard—you're tired because you've been carrying emotional weight since you were 10 years old.

Your body grew up. Your hustle grew up. But your wounds never did.

You Were Lied To: Healing Is Not Weakness

We were told that healing was soft. That talking to someone or going to therapy meant you were crazy. That conversing about feelings made you less of a man, or less strong as a woman.

So, what did we do instead?

- Fought it out
- Fuccd it away
- Drank through it
- Smoked past it
- Shut down

- Exploded on people who actually loved us

Let's tell the truth: *Suppressing emotions didn't make us strong—it made us **dangerous.** To ourselves and others.*

We hurt people who didn't deserve it.

We trusted nobody, not even ourselves.

We stayed in cycles because pain was familiar and peace felt foreign.

However, healing for a hustler *isn't* about becoming soft—it's about a different kind of hardness. It's not a spa day or any of that kind of bullshit—it's heart surgery without anesthesia. It's pulling the bullet out yourself and stitching the wound shut, knowing the scar will forever be there. This shit is serious. And it makes you dangerous in a different kind of way.

No longer to others in "the game," but to the very idea of "the game" itself. You become that ghost that *haunts* that bitch; you're the living proof that the lie is optional. Your peace is a threat. Your stability is a rebellion. You're dangerous because you can no longer be manipulated by the same triggers. You've *faced* your pain. You can't be bought with the promise of a quick "lick" or a sweet flip—you're building *real* wealth now. And you can't be intimidated by what you're putting behind you—you've already stared down the monster in the mirror and won.

Digging how powerful that is?—you're a new kind of predator now! And your prey is generational curses; your hunt is for a legacy. Your power isn't in taking a life, but in building one. And to be honest, that's a danger this kkkountry really isn't prepared for.

> *Healing? – that's Gangster. Looking yourself in the mirror and saying "I need help"? – that's power.*

What "Therapy" (or Self-Work) Really Looks Like

It looks like silence. Learning to sit in a room alone with your own thoughts and not needing a distraction, a drink, or a trigger to quiet the noise. It's trading the paranoia that kept you alive, for a vigilance that lets you live.

It also looks like grieving. Finally feeling and facing the weight of every loss you numbed yourself to—the friends buried, the time wasted, the person you used to be. It's crying for the first time in a decade—not from weakness, but from the sheer force of finally feeling something real.

And it looks like building. Not a reputation, but a routine. A legit paycheck. A savings account. A skill. It's the discipline of the grind, redirected. The same focus you used to count stacks and watch your bankroll build is now used to study, to learn, to provide without looking over your shoulder.

It's not you sitting on a stranger's couch crying every week: It's:

- Learning how to identify your emotions before they wreck your relationships
- Unlearning survival behaviors that no longer serve you
- Breaking family patterns that go back generations
- Creating boundaries your parents never taught you were allowed to
- Forgiving yourself for how you moved when you didn't know better

And it's not always deep. Sometimes healing looks like:

- Going for a walk instead of going off
- Not answering that toxic text
- Saying "no" without guilt
- Taking a nap without feeling lazy
- Choosing peace over proving a point

You don't have to be "in therapy" to start healing—but you *do* have to be honest. You *do* have to feel your shit. You *do* have to stop blaming everyone else.

You can't heal from what you can't own.

Generational Curses Aren't Spells—They're Patterns

When people talk about "breaking curses," it sounds mystical or some shit. But here's the raw truth: *A generational curse is just a behavior nobody had the courage to stop.*

- "Our family doesn't talk about emotions."
- "My father left, so I don't know how to be one."
- "My mom worked herself to death—so now I think rest is lazy."
- "We struggle, but we don't ask for help."
- "We use violence when we're hurt."
- "We cheat, we lie, we run."
- "*I* got it out the mud, so he's going to have to, too."

It gets passed down like a broken inheritance. Until somebody—*you*—says: "It *ends* here."

And let me hip you—that decision is *hard*. People will call you weird, weak, soft, different. But that's because they're still in the cycle. You?—you're walking out of it. And fucc what people have to say, anyway, you dig?

Love in a World That Doesn't Trust it

Real relationships—romantic, platonic, or familial—are built on vulnerability. But vulnerability feels like a death sentence when you're used to betrayal, setups, or loss. So, what happens? We push people away. We confuse loyalty with silence, affection with control, and distance with safety.

Signs you're disconnected emotionally:

- You shut down instead of opening up.
- You don't know how to receive love, only how to protect yourself from it.
- You expect people to leave, so you never let them get close.

We can't build lasting relationships if we're still living emotionally guarded. We can't raise children, love a partner, or show up for a friend while emotionally dissociating from everything that hurts. That's not protection—it's avoidance.

The walls we build to keep pain out also keep healing away.

Healing Is Slow—Stay with It Anyway

Healing isn't some six-week challenge with a medal at the end. It isn't a "make-a-wish" moment where all the pain evaporates because you snapped your fingers or posted the right quote online. Healing is grimy work. It's ugly crying when nobody's around. It's admitting you were wrong when pride tells you to double down. It's unlearning habits you thought were survival, but really were chains.

It's relapsing into old patterns and having to forgive yourself enough to try again tomorrow. It's the courage to face memories you buried because they hurt too much, and the patience to sit with emotions you used to numb out of existence.

But every time you choose peace over chaos, every time you tell the truth instead of hiding it, every time you lean into growth instead of running from it—you win a small battle. And those battles add up. Slowly. Quietly. But they add up.

Healing isn't about becoming perfect—it's about becoming whole. And in that process, you slowly start turning into the person your childhood self desperately needed—someone whom is safe, consistent, and free. That transformation doesn't just honor the adolescent version of you; it prepares the ground for the future family you dream about. The generational curses don't get to write the script anymore—you do.

Here's the thing: you don't owe anyone a flawless version of yourself—not your partner, not your parents, not the people who doubted you. What you owe is to *yourself*—to give yourself the chance to finally live *free*. *Free* from cycles. *Free* from masks. *Free* from the weight of everything that tried to *break* you...

So, stay with the process; even when you feel like nothing is changing, you're still not the same person whom first decided to try. You're stronger, softer, sharper, freer. Healing is slow. But so is building anything that lasts...

Community or Competition?

"The streets" teach us to see everyone as competition—someone's always trying to take your spot, your plug, your reputation. But *real* community—*true support*—is built on *mutual investment*, not *power plays*.

In hustling culture, we admire "loyalty," but we rarely practice it in its fullest form. Loyalty isn't just about showing up in conflict; it's about checking on people in silence, celebrating growth, and holding each other accountable without ego.

If everyone around you only knows the hustler version of you, ask yourself: *Do they really know you at all?* And more importantly, do they care about who you're trying to become—or only who you were?

> *The people who only know your pain might not be able to handle your healing.*

Mental Unwellness: The Silent Killer

Depression. Anxiety. PTSD (perpetually traumatic stress and despair). Anger. Detachment. These aren't weaknesses—they're symptoms of unprocessed trauma. And in hustling culture, they're everywhere. But instead of therapy, we self-medicate. Instead of healing, we hustle harder.

Why? Because "the game" doesn't leave space for emotions. You're expected to hold it down even when everything's falling apart. But that pressure breaks people—quietly, slowly, and sometimes permanently.

Mental health stigma sounds like:

- "I don't need therapy, I just need to get my bag."
- "Talking won't change what happened."
- "I ain't weak—I handle my own problems / shit."

But here's the truth: even the strongest people crack when they carry too much for too long.

> *Seeking help isn't weakness – it's a survival skill. A long-term one.*

A lot of people in this kkkountry confuse "mental unwellness" with the more commonly-used terms "mental illness" and "mental health." But there are distinct differences.

"Mental illness" is more clearly defined as those clinically diagnosable conditions that significantly impair a person's ability to function in daily life. These conditions affect your mood, your thinking, and your behavior—often requiring lifelong "management" via medication, therapy, and ongoing "support." Common examples include bipolar disorder, schizophrenia, major depressive disorder, and generalized anxiety disorder.

Key characteristics:

- **Chronic or Episodic Nature:** Mental illness can be persistent or occur in cycles, as seen in bipolar disorder.
- **Impact on Functioning:** They disrupt daily activities, relationships, and work.
- **Clinical Diagnosis:** Mental illnesses are diagnosed using "standard criteria."
- **Need for Treatment:** They often require a combination of, again, medication, therapy, and ongoing support.

"Mental unwellness," on the other hand, refers to *temporary* states of emotional or psychological distress that arise from life's challenges. *Everyone* experiences mental unwellness at some point, whether due to grief, stress, or significant life changes. Us in "the game"—and Black and Brown people in this kkkountry, generally—just seemingly experience it a little more than the rest.

Key characteristics of mental unwellness:

- **Universal Experience:** Mental unwellness affects everyone at some point.
- **Temporary Nature:** It's usually situational and resolves with time or lifestyle changes.
- **No Clinical Diagnosis Required:** Unlike mental illness, mental unwellness doesn't meet the criteria for a "formal" diagnosis.

- **Improved Through Self-Care and Time:** Shit often improves with sleep, exercise, social connection, and better stress management.

Understand the difference—and use this information to help you heal. All the while not allowing anyone to further attempt to stigmatize you with some bullshit diagnosis talking about "mental health" or "mental illness" when the terms don't fit your situation.

Creating New Norms in Old Spaces

Change won't come from outside the culture—it has to start *within* it. That means:

- Talking about emotions with people you trust.
- Checking in on friends who act "too strong."
- Normalizing therapy, coaching, or spiritual guidance.
- Breaking cycles of silence and shame.

Just imagine a culture where men can say they're hurting without being clowned. Where women don't have to carry everyone else's pain to prove their strength. Where healing is just as respected as hustling.

That's not soft. That's revolutionary.

The Strength to Feel

If "the game" has taught us anything, it's how to endure. But real strength isn't endurance—it's evolution. It's being brave enough to feel again. To speak honestly. To rebuild trust. To look in the mirror and say: *I'm more than what I had to survive.*

Your mental wellness *matters*. Your relationships *matter*. Your family and community *need* you! *Not* just alive—but *emotionally present!* It's time to take the mask off.

Because what comes after survival is *connection*. And without that, all you're doing is dying slower.

SETTING UP CHAPTER 9

Once you start healing, something wild happens: You want to give back. Not because you're trying to prove something—but because you finally have something real to offer.

In Chapter 9, we talk about legacy:

- Mentorship
- Showing up for the next generation
- Giving "game" without the trauma
- Rebuilding the community you once survived

You don't just leave "the game" behind—you leave *breadcrumbs* so others can follow a new path, too.

Because healed people don't just live differently—*they lead differently*.

Chapter 9

Mentorship, Leadership, and Leaving "The Streets" Better Than You Found Them

Let's make something clear: "The streets" didn't raise you—they *wounded* you. You *survived* them.

And if you're reading this now, it means you're finally in a place to stop surviving and start *leading*.

But not in the old way—not as the loudest voice in the room. Not as the OG with the flash and the fear. Not as the cat they respect because they know you'll crash out if "disrespected."

This ain't that kind of leadership.

This is the *healed* kind. The kind that *listens*, that uplifts. That *teaches without flexing*. That *shows young cats "the game" without feeding them to it*.

If your story ends with you getting out, that's survival. If your story creates new exits for others, that's **legacy**.

You Don't Have to Be a Saint to Lead

Let's kill this bullshit right now: You *don't* need a degree! You *don't* need a suit! You *don't* need a clean past to be a mentor and/or to leave "the streets" better than you found them!

What you need is *truth*!

- Your *truth* about what "the game" really costs.
- Your *truth* about how empty it feels when the high fades.
- Your *truth* about the nights you cried alone, too ashamed to call anyone.
- Your *truth* about what healing *really* takes.
- Your *truth* about how you were *isolated* and *alone* even at your highest, greatest, most "successful" levels.

Young people don't need perfection; they need *proof* that someone made it out and didn't forget how hard it was.

---

*They need **you**. Not the version you had to perform.*
*The version you became when you **stopped** performing.*

But Stop Selling Cats the Lie *You* Survived

Too many so-called "leaders" are still glorifying the same life that *almost killed them*. How fuccin insane is that?

They post war stories with no scars.

They talk hustle, but never mention therapy.

They call it "getting money," but don't tell the kids about the funerals, federal indictments, or the years lost to time.

If you're healed, stop selling the pain like it was a prize. Tell the *whole* truth:

- The moments you thought about giving up.
- The people you lost to pride, to bullets, to prison.
- The birthdays you missed and the children who stopped calling you "Daddy" or "Mama" because you weren't there.

- The nights you couldn't sleep because every car slowing down outside felt like a death sentence or the feds about to kick in your door.
- The betrayals and bullshit by some of your "closest" confidantes.
- The way your body still jumps at loud noises even though you're "out of the game."

Don't just give them the highlight reel. Give them the nights you cried alone in a room that smelled like mildew, dead roaches, and regret. Give them the hospital visits and the silence after a close friend's casket closed.

Because if you survived, your testimony isn't supposed to be an advertisement—it's supposed to be a warning. Your story can save somebody—but only if you tell it without the lies.

Transforming "the Hood"

Ain't no magic wand for this shit. "The hood" is more than just concrete, corners, and crack sales—it's a mindset. A cycle. A trauma passed down like a fuccd-up inheritance. To change it, you got to start with the foundation—rebuilding it physically, economically, and spiritually.

First, **reclaim the space.** "The hood" ain't just where we hustle—it's where we live, where our children play, where our elders sit on porches and stoops watching generations repeat the same mistakes. If *we* don't own it, *somebody else will*—pig police, "gentrifiers," slumlords, or the next young cat with a foolish dream of being the next Pablo.

- **Clean it up.** Organize community clean-ups. Get the waste out the gutters, paint over the bullet holes, plant some flowers and/or community gardens where the fiends used to smoke and/or nod off. (And pressure "landlords" to fix all the broken shit inside and around their properties while you're at it.) Sounds small, but when people see pride in their surroundings, they start giving a damn.

- **Repurpose the blocks / corners.** Instead of letting it be a trap spot, turn it into a community spot and resource hub. Cookouts, barbershop debates, pop-up job fairs, free food drives, voter registration, mentorship meetups. Show the young cats and kittens there's more to "the hood" than that bullshit they show on "the news."

- **Protect it.** Not with artillery—although the history of this kkkountry *does* show us that we *do* need arms against those that will attempt to burn our shit down out of jealousy and envy masked as (let's just call it) "mainstream outrage" of one kind or another—but with *unity* this time. Form neighborhood watches (*not* snitch squads!) to de-escalate beefs and protect the vulnerable, especially looking out for the youngins so they don't get sucked into dumb shit like we did.

Nevertheless, none of this works if we don't change the economics—"the hood" stays toxic because poverty keeps it on life support. So, we also have to:

- **Demand local investment.** Pressure city officials for better-resourced schools, rec centers, and job training—not just more pig policing.

- **Support Black and Brown businesses.** Buy from "the hood" *first*. If *we* don't circulate our *own* bread like *other* communities do, then *who* will?

- **Take ownership of the land.** Pool funds to buy abandoned and/or rundown properties and revitalize them. Furthermore, understand that rent-to-own programs keep wealth *in* the community, so rent and sell to *our own* whenever reasonably possible—even at a "homegrown discount."

Transforming Hearts and Minds

You can't force change, of course, but you can *inspire* it—all the young cats and kittens need to see, sometimes, is a new version of success.

And understand, also, that you can't save everybody, but you can plant those seeds. The ones who look up to you? They're watching *everything*. You telling them to "go to school" while still flexing the old life?—cats are going to follow what you *do*, not what you *say*. So:

- **Lead by example.** If you've really left "the streets," *live* like it. Ain't no "former" about it if you're still glorifying the past. As I've stressed more than a time or two, talk about the *lessons*, not the *glory*. If you're preaching and teaching "get out the game," your lifestyle can't still scream "I miss it." I can't reiterate this enough!—be honest about the costs of "the game." The funerals. The indictments. Lost time with your loved ones. PTSD. And on and on and on and on we could go.

- **Listen more than you preach.** These young cats and kittens aren't stupid—they're just traumatized. They need guidance, not lectures, however. Ask *them* what *they* want out of life before telling them what you *think* they should want. Many of these young cats just need *one* adult to take them seriously. *Be* that adult.

- **Redirect hustle energy.** The same focus that makes them a potential "problem" in "the streets"—you know, the same skills that made you a good hustler: grind mentality, loyalty, problem-solving, a seeming-sense of "no fear"—can make them a CEO. Help them pivot like you did. Redirect that energy by exposing them to more than the "street shit": field trips to colleges, tech bootcamps, or even other cities showing them that there's a bigger world outside of "the hood."

But real talk? You can't change someone who doesn't want to change. Some cats just have to hit rock bottom or learn things "the hard way." Some cats and kittens are too deep in the fog. You can't really stress or worry about them—just pour into those whom are reachable when you're reaching. For the others, your job is to be there when they're ready to put the bullshit behind them. Because you can't drown trying to save everyone, and most importantly, you have to protect your peace and the peace of those whom you *can* help save themselves.

Legal Livelihoods & Community Support

"The system" wants us to believe the only way for us to thrive is via sports, rap, or crime—that's bullshit. One of the biggest lies "the streets" help to propagate is that those are the only ways for *us* to consider ourselves as having "made it." But nah, outside the accepted bullshit of somehow "entertaining" the mainstream of amerikkka, "the game" just seems the easiest way when you don't have a blueprint for something better. Simply put, we've just got to create our *own* lanes, and here's how we can do that:

- **Start small, but think big.** Put your bread into low-capital businesses that are always in demand like barbering or the beauty industry or even food trucks—and/or those that take minimal startup capital yet bring maximum profit like pressure washing or detailing services. These are just examples; use the same creative mind that helped you navigate "the streets" to come up with something unique, bold, and needed. Can you dig it?

- **Pool resources and build together with likeminded individuals.** We might not have the capital alone, but us together?—we can fund small businesses, buy property, create co-ops, and form investment circles to assist transforming the economy in and around the neighborhood and our city. This also helps to keep the profits in "the hood."

- **Teach financial literacy.** Too many cats get a little bread and the first thing they do is blow it on chains and rentals instead of on appreciating assets. But with knowledge comes power, and in teaching budgeting, credit repair, and investing basics, you can empower cats to make wiser decisions.

- **Partner strategically with organizations that ain't on bullshit.** Work with non-exploitative organizations (you'll be able to peep the difference!) that actually *help* and are not just around to collect grant money. Partner with (*righteous!*—*not* racist!) unions for free and/or paid apprenticeships in trades such as culinary arts, HVAC installation and repair, plumbing, and in becoming an electrician. There are (unbelievably!) even some corporations out there with real community programs that are not just PR stunts that believe in hiring locally and paying fair wages in the hood where they're getting money. Seek them out.

Legacy Over Clout

Understand that "the streets" will love you until they swallow you. But real leadership means building something that lasts longer than your reputation. It ain't about being the hardest—it's about making it easier for the next man to survive without being a statistic.

The real measure of a leader isn't how many people fear you—it's how many people truly *thrive* because of you. "The hood" won't change overnight, but every cleaned-up lot, every young mind awakened, every legal dollar earned is a step toward freedom. Because "the streets" don't run / own us—*we* run / own them. And it's time to revitalize and rebuild.

Remember, "the hood" doesn't have to be a graveyard—it can be a foundation. But that starts with *us*.

Chapter 10

Rewriting Your "Rep"—Self, Spirit, and the New You

The hardest part of leaving "the game" isn't letting go of the money—it's letting go of the *identity* that comes with it.

The name you built in the streets.

The armor you wore to survive.

The myth you became to others when you didn't even know who you were to yourself.

When the noise quiets—when there's no more chase, no more fear, no more flex—you're left face-to-face with the question: *Who am I without the hustle?*

This chapter is about answering that question honestly—and using that answer to build a new life rooted in truth, not trauma.

The Hustle Built a Mask, Not a Mirror

In "the streets," identity is shaped by reputation—you become what people say about you. You move like a character in a story you didn't even write. Strong. Silent. Dangerous. Always ten steps ahead. Untouchable. Unbothered. Unfeeling.

But behind the mask?

- You might feel *lost*.
- You might carry *guilt* for things you did to survive.
- You might feel *empty* without the rush.

- You might struggle to trust peace when you finally find it.

This isn't weakness—it's humanity. But you can't heal what you won't acknowledge. And you can't become your true self if you're still hiding behind your past self's shadow.

Reclaiming Your Name

When you shed an old identity, there's a grieving process. That persona protected you. It helped you *survive*. But now you need something deeper—something that doesn't rely on fear, performance, or pain.

Ask yourself:

- What do I believe in now?
- What kind of man / woman / father / mother / friend am I trying to become?
- What do I want my name to *mean* in the next chapter of my life?

This is where your real power lives. Not in your reputation, but in *your definition*—how *you* see yourself when nobody's watching.

Community: From Territory to Tribe

In "the game," community often looks like *turf*, not *trust*. Loyalty is tested in crisis, but rarely nurtured in peace. So, when you step out of that life, many of the relationships built in the chaos won't follow you into clarity.

That's cool, though; not everyone is meant to walk with you through every season. Simply put, some will naturally fall by the wayside, and some you'll actually have to purposely put behind you. And there's nothing wrong with that. Don't consider it as being disloyal to those that helped you survive "the game" and thrive through the hustle, but instead as being loyal to *yourself* and the next chapter of your life.

Because the next chapter will require *new* community—people whom see your *future* and not just your *past*. People whom:

- Speak life into your vision.
- Challenge your blind spots with love.
- Walk with integrity, not just intensity.

And you may need to *build* this tribe. Through recovery groups. Spiritual circles. Business networks. Men's / women's groups. Therapy. Real friendship.

You don't need a crowd – you need a circle.

A Spiritual Shift (Even If You Don't Call It That)

You don't have to be religious to feel the shift. Call it God, the Universe, higher self, intuition, purpose. Whatever name you give it, the transformation from hustle to healing almost always comes with a spiritual awakening.

That voice inside you? The one that told you, *"There's more to life than this"*—that's not weakness; that's your *soul* speaking.

Tapping into that source—through prayer, through meditation, silence, nature, art, or service—rewires how you see yourself. It humbles the ego and empowers the real you. It reminds you that you're not just a product of struggle—you're a vessel for change.

The same fire that once burned you can now fuel you
*– **if** you choose to direct it inward.*

Know in your heart and mind that this shift isn't about rules or rituals—it's about recognizing that you're bigger than the survival you were born into, and that there's something greater guiding you forward.

Defining Success in Your *Own* Language

Understand, you *don't* have to chase the same goals the world sold you; "success" isn't only the money, the cars, the followers, the applause. Success can be defined on your *own* terms—in ways that *heal* you:

- Peace in your home.
- Presence with your children.
- Purpose in your work.
- Honesty in your relationships.
- Rest in your spirit.

That's wealth. That's freedom. That's power.

Peep that when you shift the definition, you shift the destination. You stop running in circles, chasing validation that doesn't last, and start building a foundation that no one can take away.

FINAL WORD: THE NAME YOU CARRY, THE LIFE YOU LEAD

You were never just the hustler. You were the strategist, the protector, the visionary, the survivor. Now it's time to *own those same gifts* in a life that doesn't drain your soul to use them.

Recognize fully that you don't need permission to evolve. You don't need to explain your healing. You just need to *walk in it*, day by day, moment by moment.

This isn't reinvention—it's remembrance. You're not becoming someone new. You're becoming who you were *before* the world told you to survive at any cost.

"The streets" may have named you one thing, but your spirit knows another. And the name you carry from this point forward will not just be about where you've been, but about where you're going and what you're building.

Know that this book was never about glorifying "the game," but instead about telling the truth—about what it gives, what it takes, and what it costs. But more than that, it was about possibility. About the fact that your story doesn't have to end in a cell, in a casket, or in regret. You can pivot. You can heal. You can rewrite your rep and your rap. Not tomorrow, not someday—today.

Because at the end of it all, legacy isn't built in "the streets" or in "the game"—it's built in the lives you touch, the love you give, and the peace you protect. That's the new hustle. That's the real win. And it's not a "game."

So, the next chapter?

That's *yours* to write.

Shall peace be unto you…

Epilogue

A Call to Arms

If you've made it this far, understand this: you didn't just read a book—you took in a transmission. *Game 4 $ale: The Hustler's Bible* isn't about me. It's about you. It's about not just surviving, but truly thriving. It's about waking up to the fact that although no one is coming to save us—we still rise, because the "game" *in* us is stronger than "the system" *around* us. And if you're holding this book, it means you've made it through the noise. Through the nights that almost broke you. Through the weight of decisions made or contemplated in desperation, fear, or pride. Through the mask you wear or wore so well, even when it hurts to keep it on.

You survived.

Again, though, this book was never just about survival. This was a blueprint for freedom. Not the kind stamped by "the system," or co-signed by "the streets"—but the kind that lets you wake up without fear, sleep without guilt, and move through this world with a clear heart and a clean name.

My thoughts, words, and actions have never been to glorify "the game," but to redefine and refocus our hustle. Hustling isn't chasing quick money or cheap thrills—it's about creating strategy where none exists, turning pressure into diamonds, and refusing to let circumstances dictate your worth.

I've paid a heavy price to learn these lessons. Too heavy, at times. But what I went through doesn't have to be repeated if the next cat up like you takes heed. So, if you walk away from these pages with nothing else, walk away with this: *your mind is your strongest hustle, and your soul and peace are not for sale*. Protect them at all costs.

To the ones thinking about getting in: "the game" (as we know it) has no retirement plan. The only guaranteed exit is either death or a plea deal. "The streets" don't love you back, and the money you're chasing isn't a "god" to be worshipped and killed over.

To the ones already in: If you keep moving in the same direction, you're headed towards the wall. You can slow down now, or you can crash and hope you live to tell about it. But understand—every day you stay, you're making it harder to walk away with your freedom, your health, or your sanity intact.

And to the ones who made it out, already: don't glamorize the hell you barely escaped. Be real enough to tell the next generation that it cost you more than you ever got back. Don't be the reason someone steps into the same fire thinking they'll come out smelling like cologne.

Other than that, you don't owe "the game" *shit*—you *gave* it enough. Your time. Your peace. Your youth. Your energy. Your potential. It's time to take that all back and reinvest it in something bigger: *you*.

This is a *war*—not against others, but against the false version of yourself that keeps trying to drag you back into survival mode.

The real enemy isn't "the hood"—it's hopelessness.

It's the belief that you can't change for the better.

It's the lie that says this is all you'll ever be.

Overcome "the game."

Not just by walking away from it—but by *building something stronger* than it ever was and/or ever gave you. By *breaking cycles*. By *creating stability*. By *choosing life* when death seemed like the only door.

You're not a statistic. You're not a myth. You're not a villain. You're the author of a new chapter—in your life and the lives of everyone whom comes *after* you.

Make it count.

When I come home, I don't just want to be free—I wish to see the seeds planted from this book grow into something bigger than all of us. Into families that stand strong. Into communities that refuse to fold. Into a generation that learns how to win without destroying itself in the process.

So, use this "game." Apply it. Share it. Live it. Don't let it sit on a shelf gathering dust—let it move through your actions, your words, your plans, your legacy.

The hustle continues—but so does the hope…

Kamaj Tawhid

Acknowledgments

To my family – thank you for holding me down through it all, especially through this wrongful conviction I'm still fighting. No names needed; if you've been there, you know. And to my brother – welcome home, man. Twenty-six years from 18 to 45... nobody deserved that burden – and surely not you!!! Love you, always.

Much love to my Tennessee and California M4v3n families – the ones who kept me grounded and motivated: Big Monsta, Matt Movin, Lil Delo, Blue Demon, C Fo, Cash Flow, Gangsta Grimm, Dee Smilz, Wacco, Babylon, TearDrop, Choppa, Money Baggs, Baby Ray Ray, Tre Money, Snoop, Tiny Madroc, Tragic Tre, C-Lo, Devo, Cinbad, GhostTown, Big Madroc, and Tiny Dopey.

To the homies who helped me stay focused while fighting and writing *Game 4 $ale: The Hustler's Bible* – Monsta Deuce, Tray Avalon, R30, LC, Sep, Croug, Glocc 40, Hoova Joe, RattMan, Big Doocie Loc, J Blue, Wiccd 60, Fig, RollX, Harlem Mike, Chucc40, JT, T Gunn, CCuz, Danger, Goonie Grape, Tanc, and Hoova Scott – I appreciate you all for keeping my head in the game.

Respect to Dr. Larry Monk and Carlos Parks of *Fifth Sun TV* – along with executive producer Senita Jae – for giving my story a platform through documentary *This is Amerikkka: The Kenneth Deangelo Thomas Story*. In addition, producer Jerome Moore, for having me on podcast *Deep Dish Conversations*. You all helped the world see the truth behind my continued incarceration.

To my sisters and brothers at *Inside Out Outreach Consultants* – President Shawn'a Hatcher, Quinton "Bo Pete" Sanders, Rivera L. Peoples, Vice President LaPorcsha Peoples, Kenneth A. "Ken Ken" Brown, Jr., Terry Tyrone "Ali" Smith, Brother Fahim, and Brother Mitch – thank you for helping me stay locked into the bigger struggle.

To Janet Wolf, Shawn Whitsell, Amy Barnes, Andy Watts, Abu-Ali Abdur-Rahman, Jasper Lewis, Shawn Stafford, and Nun Tuam of *SALT* (School for Alternative Learning and Transformation) – you've kept my mind growing and sharp. (But I still think Abigail did the most harm!)

Deep gratitude to Dawn Deaner of the *Choosing Justice Initiative* and Chanell Arnold-Murray of *AK Investigations* for your work proving my innocence. To anyone out there fighting bogus charges or constitutional violations: these are real Souljas who can stand beside you.

Salute to the legal warriors who keep me inspired: E.J. Harbison, Ken Parnell, Thomas Clardy, the eternal asshole Bobby Nash, and attorneys Eileen M. Parrish and Jeffrey O. Powell. You remind me why the fight must go on.

And finally – a big middle finger to former assistant district attorney Lisa Angela Naylor, and to the Davidson County (Tennessee) District Attorney's Office and Metro-Nashville Police Department for hiding the evidence of my innocence for over twenty-five years. I mean this from my soul: may you all burn in hell for what you've done – to me, to my brother, and to countless others. Same goes for late "judge" Seth Norman, the Davidson County Criminal Courts, collectively, and the Tennessee Board of Professional Responsibility, for letting this injustice stand unchecked. More on that coming soon…

The struggle continues…

Recommended Reading

- *The Unapologectic Guide to Black Mental Health: Navigate an Unequal System, Learn Tools for Emotional Wellness, and Get the Help You Deserve* by Rheeda Walker, Ph.D.
- *The Strong Black Woman: How a Myth Endangers the Physical and Mental Health of Black Women* by Marita Golden
- *The Millionaire Next Door: The Surprising Secrets of America's Wealthy* by Thomas J. Stanley, Ph.D. & William D. Danko, Ph.D.
- *The Psychology of Money: Timeless Lessons on Wealth, Greed, and Happiness by* Morgan Housel
- *Forty Million Dollar Slaves: The Rise, Fall, and Redemption of the Black Athlete* by William C. Rhoden
- *Cocaine Nation: How the White Trade Took Over the World* by Tom Feiling
- *Snitch: Informants, Cooperators & the Corruption of Justice* by Ethan Brown.
- *The 7 Habits of Highly Effective People* by Stephen R. Covey
- *Think and Grow Rich* by Napoleon Hill
- *The Power of Your Subconscious Mind* by Joseph Murphy
- *As a Man / Woman Thinketh* by James Allen
- *Black Love is a Revolutionary Act* by Umoja
- *Mediocre: The Dangerous Legacy of White Male Power* by Ijeoma Oluo

The Hustler's Manifesto

Game ain't free.
Life ain't fair.
Knowledge is eternal.
Don't just play "the game"—*own it*.
Don't just chase the dollar—*chase freedom*.
Never sell your soul cheap.
Every lesson is a weapon.
Every struggle is strategy.
Every setback is preparation.
Protect your mind.
Guard your spirit.
Heal your wounds.

Because the greatest hustle…
Isn't stacking paper.
It's reclaiming peace.
It's mending what was broken.
It's learning to love yourself again.

The real hustler's hustle?
Turning pain into power.
Struggle into strategy.
Lessons into legacy.
And healing into wholeness.

The next move is yours…

Kamaj Tawhid

A Talk I Had with Some Young Cats I Know

"At some point, every hustler has to make a choice: will I keep living for "the game"... or will I start building a life beyond it?

The truth is, "the game" takes too much. It drains your time, your energy, your peace. You can't give your full self to love when half of you is locked in survival mode. You can't be a steady parent when "the streets" demand you stay unpredictable.

See—"street money" can buy shoes, cars, homes, even moments of happiness. But "street money" can't buy presence. It can't buy stability. It can't buy legacy.

This isn't about rejection—it's about timing. Sometimes the best move is to pause, to heal, to step away from the chaos. Because when you finally get on your "grown man" and put "the game" behind you, you discover the greatest flex: creating a life where your children don't / won't have to carry the same weight *you* once did.

That's real love. That's real fatherhood. That's real legacy."

QUESTION: "So, are you saying hustlers shouldn't have families?"

ANSWER: "Not exactly. What I'm saying is, *timing* matters. 'The game' is chaotic—it's unstable by nature. Serious relationships, family, and children require consistency, trust, peace. You can't give that while you're still knee-deep in 'the game.'

I've witnessed far too many cats think that money makes them a provider, but provision without presence is empty. Your children don't just need some bullshit Jordans or even food on the table—they need *you*! *Fully*. And if the lifestyle threatens your freedom or your life, well... it threatens *theirs*, too.

So, my position is this: don't rush it. Don't confuse motion with progress. Put 'the game' behind you first. Build your foundation. Because when you finally walk away from 'the game,' you can give love and family something 'the streets' never could: stability, safety, and legacy…"

AUTHOR BIO

Kamaj Dakari Tawhid (known within "the system" as Kenneth Deangelo "Delo" Thomas, prisoner # 262443) is the author of *This Is Amerikkka: The Troublesome Life, Loves & Soul of a Conscientious Thug* (Still Waters Prose, 2020). Wrongly incarcerated in tennessee for over two decades, Kamaj has never stopped fighting to prove his complete innocence.

No stranger to local, national, and even international headlines, his case reflects both the deep injustices of the criminal legal system and the resilience of the human spirit. In addition to recently uncovering suppressed evidence that irrefutably proves his innocence in his original wrongful conviction, Kamaj, in late 2023, had 16 fabricated felony charges—tied to false accusations of leading a 2017 prison uprising—fully dismissed.

Despite enduring the weight of wrongful imprisonment, Kamaj's voice and vision remain unshaken. Through his writing, he not only tells his own story but also sheds light on broader issues of systemic injustice, survival, and transformation.

He continues to seek exoneration—or, in the alternative, the radical act of state accountability he calls "euthanization"—while asking for any and all support from those who believe in truth, justice, and human dignity.

To learn more about Kamaj, his ongoing fight, or ways to contribute to his cause, please visit www.FreeKamaj.org or www.KamajTawhid.com, the Delo Is Innocent Twitter page (x@TawhidKamaj), or the Justice for Kenneth D. Thomas Facebook page.

www.ingramcontent.com/pod-product-compliance
Lightning Source LLC
Chambersburg PA
CBHW020910080526
44589CB00011B/528